Metaphy

LYRICS & POEMS

OF

The Seventeenth Century

Metaphysical
LYRICS & POEMS
OF
The Seventeenth Century

DONNE to *BUTLER*

Selected and edited, with an Essay

By HERBERT J. C. GRIERSON

OXFORD UNIVERSITY PRESS

Oxford University Press, Walton Street, Oxford OX2 6DP

OXFORD LONDON GLASGOW
NEW YORK TORONTO MELBOURNE WELLINGTON
NAIROBI DAR ES SALAAM CAPE TOWN
KUALA LUMPUR SINGAPORE JAKARTA HONG KONG TOKYO
DELHI BOMBAY CALCUTTA MADRAS KARACHI

ISBN 0 19 881102 0

First published by the Clarendon Press 1921
First issued as an Oxford University Press paperback 1959
This reprint 1979

Printed in Great Britain by J. W. Arrowsmith Ltd., Bristol

CONTENTS.

DIVINE POEMS.

MISCELLANIES.

Elegies, Epistles, Satires, and Meditations.

INTRODUCTION.

I

Metaphysical Poetry, in the full sense of the term, is a poetry which, like that of the *Divina Commedia*, the *De Natura Rerum*, perhaps Goethe's *Faust*, has been inspired by a philosophical conception of the universe and the rôle assigned to the human spirit in the great drama of existence. These poems were written because a definite interpretation of the riddle, the atoms of Epicurus rushing through infinite empty space, the theology of the schoolmen as elaborated in the catechetical disquisitions of St. Thomas, Spinoza's vision of life *sub specie aeternitatis*, beyond good and evil, laid hold on the mind and the imagination of a great poet, unified and illumined his comprehension of life, intensified and heightened his personal consciousness of joy and sorrow, of hope and fear, by broadening their significance, revealing to him in the history of his own soul a brief abstract of the drama of human destiny. 'Poetry is the first and last of all knowledge—it is as immortal as the heart of man.' Its themes are the simplest experiences of the surface of life, sorrow and joy, love and battle, the peace of the country, the bustle and stir of towns, but equally the boldest conceptions, the profoundest intuitions, the subtlest and most complex classifications and 'discourse of reason', if into these too the poet can 'carry sensation', make of them passionate experiences communicable in vivid and moving imagery, in rich and varied harmonies.

It is no such great metaphysical poetry as that of Lucretius and Dante that the present essay deals with, which this volume seeks to illustrate. Of the poets from whom it culls, Donne is familiar with the definitions and distinctions of Mediaeval Scholasticism; Cowley's bright and alert, if not profound mind, is attracted by the achievements of science and the systematic materialism of Hobbes. Donne, moreover, is metaphysical not only in virtue of his scholasticism, but by his deep reflective interest in the experiences of which his poetry is the expression, the new psychological curiosity with which he writes of love and religion. The divine poets who follow Donne have each the inherited metaphysic, if one may so call it, of the Church to which he is attached, Catholic or Anglican. But none of the poets has for his main theme a metaphysic like that of Epicurus or St. Thomas passionately apprehended and imaginatively expounded. Donne, the most thoughtful and imaginative of them all, is more aware of disintegration than of comprehensive harmony, of the clash between the older physics and metaphysics on the one hand and the new science of Copernicus and Galileo and Vesalius and Bacon on the other:

The new philosophy calls all in doubt,
The element of fire is quite put out;
The sun is lost and the earth, and no man's wit
Can well direct him where to look for it.
And freely men confess that this world's spent,
When in the planets and the firmament
They seek so many new; they see that this
Is crumbled out again to his atomies.

Have not all souls thought
For many ages that our body is wrought
Of air and fire and other elements?
And now they think of new ingredients;
And one soul thinks one, and another way
Another thinks, and 'tis an even lay.

The greatest English poet, indeed, of the century was, or believed himself to be, a philosophical or theological poet of the same order as Dante. *Paradise Lost* was written to be a justification of 'the ways of God to men', resting on a theological system as definite and almost as carefully articulated in the *De Doctrina Christiana* as that which Dante had accepted from the *Summa* of Aquinas. And the poet embodied his argument in a dramatic poem as vividly and intensely conceived, as magnificently and harmoniously set forth, as the *Divina Commedia*. But in truth Milton was no philosopher. The subtleties of theological definition and inference eluded his rationalistic, practical, though idealistic, mind. He proved nothing. The definitely stated argument of the poem is an obvious begging of the question. What he did was to create, or give a new definiteness and sensible power to, a great myth which, through his poem, continued for a century or more to dominate the mind and imagination of pious protestants without many of them suspecting the heresies which lurked beneath the imposing and dazzling poem in which was retold the Bible story of the fall and redemption of man.

Metaphysical in this large way, Donne and his followers to Cowley are not, yet the word describes better what is the peculiar quality of their poetry than any other, e.g. fantastic, for poetry may be fantastic in so many different ways, witness Skelton and the Elizabethans, and Hood and Browning. It lays stress on the right things—the survival, one might say the reaccentuation, of the metaphysical strain, the *concetti metafisici ed ideali* as Testi calls them in contrast to the simpler imagery of classical poetry, of mediaeval Italian poetry; the more intellectual, less verbal, character of their wit compared with the conceits of the Elizabethans; the finer psychology of which their conceits are often the expression; their learned imagery; the argumentative, subtle evolution of their lyrics; above all the peculiar blend of passion and thought, feeling and ratiocination which is their greatest achievement. Passionate thinking is always apt to become metaphysical, probing and investigating the experience from which it takes its rise. All these qualities are in the poetry of Donne, and Donne is the great master of English poetry in the seventeenth century.

The Italian influence which Wyatt and Surrey brought into English poetry at the Renaissance gave it a more serious, a more thoughtful colour. They caught, especially Wyatt in some of the finest of his sonnets and songs, that spirit of 'high seriousness' which Chaucer with all his admiration of Italian poetry had failed to apprehend. English mediaeval poetry is often gravely pious, haunted by the fear of death and the judgement, melancholy over the 'Falls of Princes'; it is never serious and thoughtful in the introspective, reflective, dignified manner which it became in Wyatt and Sackville, and our 'sage and serious' Spenser, and in the songs of the first group of Elizabethan courtly poets, Sidney and Raleigh and Dyer. One has but to recall 'My lute, awake! perform the last', 'Forget not yet the tried intent', 'My mind to me a kingdom is', and to contrast them in mind with the songs which Henry VIII and Cornish were still composing and singing when Wyatt began to write, in order to realize what Italy and the Renaissance did to deepen the strain of English lyric poetry as that had flowed under French influence from the thirteenth to the sixteenth centuries. But French influence, the influence of Ronsard and his fellows, renewed itself in the seventies, and the great body of Elizabethan song is as gay and careless and impersonal as the earlier lyric had been, though richer in colour and more varied in rhythm. Then came Donne and Jonson (the schoolman and the classical scholar, one might say, emphasizing for the moment single aspects of their work), and new qualities of spirit and form were given to lyrical poetry, and not to lyrical poetry alone.

In dealing with poets who lived and wrote before the eighteenth century we are always confronted with the difficulty of recovering the personal, the biographical element, which, if sometimes disturbing and disconcerting, is yet essential to a complete understanding of their work. Men were not different from what they are now, and if there be hardly a lyric of Goethe's or Shelley's that does not owe something to the accidents of their lives, one may feel sure it was in varying degrees the same with poets three hundred years ago. Poems are not written by influences or movements or sources, but come from the living hearts of men. Fortunately, in the case of Donne, one of the most individual of poets, it is possible to some extent to reproduce the circumstances, the inner experiences from which his intensely personal poetry flowed.

He was in the first place a Catholic. Our history text-books make so little of the English Catholics that one is apt to forget they existed and were, for themselves at any rate, not a political problem, but real and suffering individuals. 'I had my first breeding and conversation', says Donne, 'with men of a suppressed and afflicted religion, accustomed to the despite of death and hungry of an imagined martyrdom.' In these circumstances, we gather, he was carefully and religiously educated, and after some years at Oxford and Cambridge was taken or sent abroad, perhaps with a view to entering foreign service, more probably with a view to the priesthood, and visited Italy and Spain. And then, one conjectures, a reaction took place, the rebellion of a full-blooded, highly intellectual temperament against a superimposed bent. He entered the Inns of Court in 1592, at the age of nineteen, and flung himself into the life of a student and the life of a young man about town, Jack Donne, 'not dissolute but very neat, a great visitor of ladies, a great frequenter of plays, a great writer of conceited verses'. 'Neither was it possible that a vulgar soul should dwell in such promising features.' He joined the band of reckless and raffish young men who sailed with Essex to Cadiz and the Islands. He was taken into the service of Sir Thomas Egerton. Ambition began to vie with the love of pleasure, when a hasty marriage closed a promising career, and left him bound in shallows and in miseries, to spend years in the suitorship of the great, and to find at last, not altogether willingly, a haven in the Anglican priesthood, and reveal himself as the first great orator that Church produced.

The record of these early years is contained in Donne's satires—harsh, witty, lucid, full of a young man's scorn of fools and low callings, and a young thinker's consciousness of the problems of religion in an age of divided faiths, and of justice in a corrupt world—and in his Love Songs and Sonnets and Elegies. The satires were more generally known; the love poems the more influential in courtly and literary circles.

Donne's genius, temperament, and learning gave to his love poems certain qualities which immediately arrested attention and have given them ever since a power at once fascinating and disconcerting despite the faults of phrasing and harmony which, for a century after Dryden, obscured, and to some still outweigh, their poetic worth. The first of these is a depth and range of feeling unknown to the majority of Elizabethan sonneteers and song-writers. Over all the Elizabethan sonnets, in greater or less measure, hangs the suggestion of translation or imitation. Watson, Sidney, Daniel, Spenser, Drayton, Lodge, all of them, with rarer or more frequent touches of individuality, are pipers of Petrarch's woes, sighing in the strain of Ronsard or more often of Desportes. Shakespeare, indeed, in his great sequence, and Drayton in at any rate one sonnet, sounded a deeper note, revealed a fuller sense of the complexities and contradictions of passionate devotion. But Donne's treatment of love is entirely unconventional except when he chooses to dally half ironically with the convention of Petrarchian adoration. His songs are the expression in unconventional, witty language of all the moods of a lover that experience and imagination have taught him to understand—sensuality aerated by a brilliant wit; fascination and scornful anger inextricably blended:

When by thy scorn, O murdress, I am dead
And that thou think'st thee free
From all solicitations from me,
Then shall my ghost come to thy bed;

the passionate joy of mutual and contented love:

All other things to their destruction draw,
  Only our love hath no decay;
This no to-morrow hath nor yesterday,
  Running it never runs from us away,
But truly keeps his first, last, everlasting day;

the sorrow of parting which is the shadow of such joy; the gentler pathos of temporary separation in married life:

Let not thy divining heart
  Forethink me any ill,
Destiny may take thy part,
  And may thy fears fulfil;
    But think that we
Are but turn'd aside to sleep;
They who one another keep
  Alive ne'er parted be;

the mystical heights and the mystical depths of love:

> Study me then you who shall lovers be
> At the next world, that is, at the next Spring:
> For I am every dead thing
> In whom love wrought new Alchemy.

If Donne had expressed this wide range of intense feeling as perfectly as he has done at times poignantly and startlingly; if he had given to his poems the same impression of entire artistic sincerity that Shakespeare conveys in the greater of his sonnets and Drayton once achieved; if to his many other gifts had been added a deeper and more controlling sense of beauty, he would have been, as he nearly is, the greatest of love poets. But there is a second quality of his poetry which made it the fashion of an age, but has been inimical to its general acceptance ever since, and that is its metaphysical wit. 'He affects the metaphysics', says Dryden, 'not only in his satires but in his amorous verses where nature only should reign; and perplexes the minds of the fair sex with nice speculations of philosophy when he should engage their hearts and entertain them with the softnesses of love.' 'Amorous verses', 'the fair sex', and 'the softnesses of love' are the vulgarities of a less poetic and passionate age than Donne's, but metaphysics he does affect. But a metaphysical strand, *concetti metafisici ed ideali*, had run through the mediaeval love-poetry of which the Elizabethan sonnets are a descendant. It had attained its fullest development in the poems of Dante and his school, had been subordinated to rhetoric and subtleties of expression rather than thought in Petrarch, and had lost itself in the pseudo-metaphysical extravagances of Tebaldeo, Cariteo, and Serafino. Donne was no conscious reviver of the metaphysics of Dante, but to the game of elaborating fantastic conceits and hyperboles which was the fashion throughout

Europe, he brought not only a full-blooded temperament and acute mind, but a vast and growing store of the same scholastic learning, the same Catholic theology, as controlled Dante's thought, jostling already with the new learning of Copernicus and Paracelsus. The result is startling and disconcerting,—the comparison of parted lovers to the legs of a pair of compasses, the deification of his mistress by the discovery that she is only to be defined by negatives or that she can read the thoughts of his heart, a thing 'beyond an angel's art'; and a thousand other subtleties of quintessences and nothingness, the mixture of souls and the significance of numbers, to say nothing of the aerial bodies of angels, the phoenix and the mandrake's root, Alchemy and Astrology, legal contracts and *non obstantes*, 'late schoolboys and sour prentices', 'the king's real and his stamped face'. But the effect aimed at and secured is not entirely fantastic and erudite. The motive inspiring Donne's images is in part the same as that which led Shakespeare from the picturesque, natural and mythological, images of *A Midsummer-Night's Dream* and *The Merchant of Venice* to the homely but startling phrases and metaphors of *Hamlet* and *Macbeth*, the 'blanket of the dark', the

fat weed
That rots itself in ease on Lethe wharf,

'the rank sweat of an enseamed bed'. It is the same desire for vivid and dramatic expression. The great master at a later period of dramatic as well as erudite pulpit oratory coins in his poems many a startling, jarring, arresting phrase:

For God's sake hold your tongue and let me love:

Who ever comes to shroud me do not harm
Nor question much
That subtle wreath of hair, which crowns my arm:

I taught my silks their rustling to forbear,
Even my opprest shoes dumb and silent were.

I long to talk with some old lover's ghost
Who died before the God of love was born;

Twice or thrice had I loved thee
Before I knew thy face or name,
So in a voice, so in a shapeless flame,
Angels affect us oft and worshipped be;

And whilst our souls negotiate there
    We like sepulchral statues lay;
All day the same our postures were
    And we said nothing all the day.

My face and brest of haircloth, and my head
With care's harsh, sudden hoariness o'er-spread.

These vivid, simple, realistic touches are too quickly merged in learned and fantastic elaborations, and the final effect of every poem of Donne's is a bizarre and blended one; but if the greatest poetry rises clear of the bizarre, the fantastic, yet very great poetry may be bizarre if it be the expression of a strangely blended temperament, an intense emotion, a vivid imagination.

What is true of Donne's imagery is true of the other disconcerting element in his poetry, its harsh and rugged verse. It is an outcome of the same double motive, the desire to startle and the desire to approximate poetic to direct, unconventional, colloquial speech. Poetry is always a balance, sometimes a compromise, between what has to be said and the prescribed pattern to which the saying of it is adjusted. In poetry such as Spenser's, the musical flow, the melody and harmony of line and stanza, is dominant, and the meaning is adjusted to it at the not infrequent cost of diffuseness—if a delightful diffuseness—and even some weakness of phrasing logically and rhetorically considered. In Shakespeare's tragedies the thought and feeling tend to break through the prescribed pattern till blank verse becomes almost rhythmical prose, the rapid overflow of the lines admitting hardly the semblance of pause. This is the kind of effect Donne is always aiming at, alike in his satires and lyrics, bending and cracking the metrical pattern to the rhetoric of direct and vehement utterance. The result is often, and to eighteenth-century ears attuned to the clear and defined, if limited, harmony of Waller and Dryden and Pope was, rugged and harsh. But here again, to those who have ears that care to hear, the effect is not finally inharmonious. Donne's verse has a powerful and haunting harmony of its own. For Donne is not simply, no poet could be, willing to force his accent, to strain and crack a prescribed pattern; he is striving to find a rhythm that will express the passionate fullness of his mind, the fluxes and refluxes of his moods; and the felicities of verse are as frequent and startling as those of phrasing. He is one of the first masters, perhaps *the* first, of the elaborate stanza or paragraph in which the discords of individual lines or phrases are resolved in the complex and rhetorically effective harmony of the whole group of lines:

If yet I have not all thy love,
Deare, I shall never have it all,
I cannot breathe one other sigh, to move,
Nor can entreat one other tear to fall,
And all my treasure, which should purchase thee,
Sighs, tears, and oaths, and letters I have spent.
Yet no more can be due to me,
Than at the bargain made was meant,
If then thy gift of love was partial,
That some to me, some shuld to others fall,
  Deare, I shall never have thee all.

But I am none; nor will my sunne renew.
You lovers for whose sake the lesser sunne
  At this time to the Goat is run
  To fetch new lust and give it you,
    Enjoy your summer all:

Since she enjoys her long night's festival,
Let me prepare towards her, and let me call
This hour her Vigil and her Eve, since this

Both the years | and the days | deep mid|night is.

The wrenching of accent which Jonson complained of is not entirely due to carelessness or indifference. It has often both a rhetorical and a harmonious justification. Donne plays with rhythmical effects as with conceits and words and often in much the same way. Mr. Fletcher Melton's interesting analysis of his verse has not, I think, established his main thesis, which like so many 'research' scholars he over-emphasizes, that the whole mystery of Donne's art lies in his use of the same sound now in *arsis*, now in *thesis*; but his examples show that this is one of many devices by which Donne secures two effects, the troubling of the regular fall of the verse stresses by the intrusion of rhetorical stress on syllables which the metrical pattern leaves unstressed, and, secondly, an echoing and re-echoing of similar sounds parallel to his fondness for resemblances in thoughts and things apparently the most remote from one another. There is, that is to say, in his verse the same blend as in his diction of the colloquial and the bizarre. He writes as one who *will* say what he has to say without regard to conventions of poetic diction or smooth verse, but what he has to say is subtle and surprising, and so are the metrical effects with which it is presented. There is nothing of unconscious or merely careless harshness in such an effect as this:

Poor soul, in this thy flesh what dost thou know?
Thou know'st thyself so little that thou knowst not
How thou didst die, nor how thou wast begot.
Thou neither know'st how thou at first camest in,
Nor how thou took'st the poison of man's sin;

> Nor dost thou though thou know'st that thou art so
> By what way thou art made immortal know.

In Donne's pronunciation, as in southern English to-day, 'thou', 'how', 'soul', 'know', 'though', and 'so' were not far removed from each other in sound and the reiterated notes ring through the lines like a tolling bell. Mr. Melton has collected, and any careful reader may discover for himself, many similar subtleties of poetical rhetoric; for Donne is perhaps our first great master of poetic rhetoric, of poetry used, as Dryden and Pope were to use it, for effects of oratory rather than of song, and the advance which Dryden achieved was secured by subordinating to oratory the more passionate and imaginative qualities which troubled the balance and movement of Donne's packed but imaginative rhetoric.

It was not indeed in lyrical verse that Dryden followed and developed Donne, but in his eulogistic, elegiac, satirical, and epistolary verse. The progress of Dryden's eulogistic style is traceable from his earliest metaphysical extravagances through lines such as those addressed to the Duchess of York, where Waller is his model, to the verses on the death of Oldham in which a more natural and classical strain has entirely superseded his earlier extravagances and elegancies. In truth Donne's metaphysical eulogies and elegies and epistles are a hard nut to crack for his most sympathetic admirers. And yet they have undeniable qualities. The metaphysics are developed in a more serious, a less paradoxical, strain than in some of the songs and elegies. In his letters he is an excellent, if far from a perfect, talker in verse; and the personality which they reveal is a singularly charming one, grave, loyal, melancholy, witty. If some of the elegiac pieces are packed with tasteless and extravagant hyperboles, the *Anniversaries* (especially the second) remains, despite all its faults, one of the greatest poems on death in the language, the fullest record in our literature of the disintegrating collision in a sensitive mind of the old tradition and the new learning. Some of the invocational passages in *Of the Progresse of the Soule* are among the finest examples of his subtle and passionate thinking as well as of his most elaborate verse rhetoric.

But the most intense and personal of Donne's poems, after the love songs and elegies, are his later religious sonnets and songs; and their influence on subsequent poetry was even more obvious and potent. They are as personal and as tormented as his earlier 'love-song weeds', for his spiritual Aeneid was a troubled one To date his conversion to Anglicanism is not easy. In his satires there is a veiled Roman tone. By 1602 he disclaims to Egerton 'all love of a corrupt religion', but in the autumn of the previous year he had been meditating a satire on Queen Elizabeth as one of the world's great heretics. His was not a conversion but a reconciliation, an acquiescence in the faith of his country, the established religion of his legal sovereign, and the act cost him some pangs. 'A convert from Popery to Protestantism,' said Dr. Johnson, 'gives up so much of what he has held as sacred as anything that he retains, there is so much laceration of mind in such a conversion, that it can hardly be sincere and lasting.' Something of that laceration of mind is discernible in Donne's religious verse:

> Show me dear Christ that spouse so bright and clear.

But the conflict between the old and the reformed faiths was not the only, nor perhaps the principal trouble for Donne's enlightened mind ready to recognize in all the Churches 'virtual beams of one sun', 'connatural pieces of one circle'. A harder fight was that between the secular, the 'man of the world' temper of his mind and the claims of a pious and ascetic calling. It was not the errors of his youth, as the good Walton supposed, which constituted the great stumbling block, though he never ignores these:

> O might those sighs and tears return again
> Into my breast and eyes, which I have spent,
> That I might in this holy discontent
> Mourn with some fruit, as I have mourned in vain.

It was rather the temperament of one who, at a time when a public career was more open to unassisted talent, might have proved an active and useful, if ambitious, civil servant, or professional man, at war with the claims of a religious life which his upbringing had taught him was incompatible with worldly ambition. George Herbert, a much more contented Anglican than Donne ever became, knew something of the same struggle before he bent his neck to the collar.

The two notes then of Donne's religious poems are the Catholic and the personal. He is the first of our Anglo-Catholic poets, and he is our first intensely personal religious poet, expressing always not the mind simply of the Christian as such, but the conflicts and longings of one troubled soul, one subtle and fantastic mind. For Donne's technique—his phrasing and conceits, the metaphysics of mediaeval Christianity, his packed verse with its bold, irregular fingering and echoing vowel sounds—remains what it had been from the outset. The echoing sounds in lines such as these cannot be quite casual:

> O might those *sighs* and tears return again
> Into my breast and *eyes*, which *I* have spent,
> That *I* might in this holy discontent
> Mourn with some fruit, as *I* have mourned in vain;

In mine *Idolat'ry* what showers of rain
Mine eyes did waste? What griefs *my* heart did rent?
That sufferance was *my* sin; now *I* repent
Cause *I* did suffer *I* must suffer pain.

In the remaining six lines the same sound never recurs.

A metaphysical, a philosophical poet, to the degree to which even his contemporary Fulke Greville might be called such, Donne was not. The thought in his poetry is not his primary concern but the feeling. No scheme of thought, no interpretation of life became for him a complete and illuminating experience. The central theme of his poetry is ever his own intense personal moods, as a lover, a friend, an analyst of his own experiences worldly and religious. His philosophy cannot unify these experiences. It represents the reaction of his restless and acute mind on the intense experience of the moment, a reading of it in the light now of one, now of another philosophical or theological dogma or thesis caught from his multifarious reading, developed with audacious paradox or more serious intention, as an expression, an illumination of that mood to himself and to his reader. Whether one choose to call him a metaphysical or a fantastic poet, the stress must be laid on the word 'poet'. Whether verse or prose be his medium, Donne is always a poet, a creature of feeling and imagination, seeking expression in vivid phrase and complex harmonics, whose acute and subtle intellect was the servant, if sometimes the unruly servant, of passion and imagination.

II

Donne's influence was felt in his own day by two strangely different classes of men, both attached by close ties to the Court. For the Court, the corrupt, ambitious, intriguing, dissolute but picturesque and dazzling court of the old pagan Elizabeth, the pedantic and drunken James, the dignified and melancholy and politically blinded Charles, was the centre round which all Donne's secular interests revolved. He can speak of it as bitterly and sardonically as Shakespeare in *Hamlet*:

> Here's no more newes, then vertue, I may as well
> Tell you Cales or St. Michael's tale for newes, as tell
> That vice doth here habitually dwell.
>
> . . . .
>
> But now 'tis incongruity to smile,
> Therefore I end; and bid farewell a while,
> *At Court*, though *From Court* were the better style.

He knows its corruptions as well as Milton and commends Lady Bedford as Milton might have commended Alice Egerton. All the same, to be shut out from the Court, in the city or the country, is to inhabit a desert, or sepulchre, for *there*:

> The Princes favour is defused o'er all,
> From which all Fortunes, Names, and Natures fall.
> And all is warmth and light and good desire.

It was among the younger generation of Courtiers that Donne found the warmest admirers of his paradoxical and sensual audacities as a love-poet, as it was the divines who looked to Laud and the Court for Anglican doctrine and discipline who revered his memory, enshrined by the pious Izaak Walton, as of a divine poet and preacher. The 'metaphysicals' were all on the King's side. Even Andrew Marvell was neither Puritan nor Republican. 'Men ought to have trusted God', was his final judgement on the Rebellion, 'they ought to have trusted the King with the whole matter'. They were on the side of the King, for they were on the side of the humanities; and the

Puritan rebellion, whatever the indirect constitutional results, was in itself and at the moment a fanatical upheaval, successful because it also threw up the John Zizka of his age; its triumph was the triumph of Cromwell's sword:

> And for the last effect
> Still keep the sword erect.
>
> Besides the force it has to fright
> The spirits of the shady night,
> The same arts that did gain
> A power must it maintain.

To call these poets the 'school of Donne' or 'metaphysical' poets may easily mislead if one takes either phrase in too full a sense. It is not only that they show little of Donne's subtlety of mind or 'hydroptic, immoderate thirst of human learning', but they want, what gives its interest to this subtle and fantastic misapplication of learning, the complexity of mood, the range of personal feeling which lends such fullness of life to Donne's strange and troubled poetry. His followers, amorous and courtly, or pious and ecclesiastical, move in a more rarefied atmosphere; their poetry is much more truly 'abstract' than Donne's, the witty and fantastic elaboration of one or two common moods, of compliment, passion, devotion, penitence. It is very rarely that one can detect a deep personal note in the delightful love-songs with which the whole period abounds from Carew to Dryden. The collected work of none of them would give such an impression of a real history behind it, a history of many experiences and moods, as Donne's Songs and Sonnets and the Elegies, and, as one must still believe, the sonnets of Shakespeare record. Like the Elizabethan sonneteers they all dress and redress the same theme in much the same manner, though the manner is not quite the Elizabethan, nor the theme. Song has superseded the sonnet, and the passion of which they sing has lost most of the Petrarchian, chivalrous strain, and become in a very definite meaning of the words, 'simple and sensuous'. And if the religious poets are rather more individual and personal, the personal note is less intense, troubled and complex than in Donne's Divine Poems; the individual is more merged in the Christian, Catholic or Anglican.

Donne and Jonson are probably in the main responsible for the unconventional purity and naturalness of their diction, for these had both 'shaken hands with' Spenserian archaism and strangeness, with the 'rhetoric' of the sonneteers and poems like *Venus and Adonis*; and their style is untouched by any foreshadowing of Miltonic diction or the jargon of a later poetic vocabulary. The metaphysicals are the masters of the 'neutral style', of a diction equally appropriate, according as it may be used, to prose and verse. If purity and naturalness of style is a grace, they deserved well of the English language, for few poets have used it with a more complete acceptance of the established tradition of diction and idiom. There are no poets till we come perhaps to Cowper, and he has not quite escaped from jargon, or Shelley, and his imagination operates in a more ethereal atmosphere, whose style is so entirely that of an English gentleman of the best type, natural, simple, occasionally careless, but never diverging into vulgar colloquialism, as after the Restoration, or into conventional, tawdry splendour, as in the century of Akenside and Erasmus Darwin. Set a poem by George Herbert beside Gray at his best, e.g.

Sweet day so cool, so calm, so bright,
The bridal of the earth and sky,
The dew shall weep thy fall to-night,
For thou must die; &c.

set that beside even a good verse from Gray, and one realizes the charm of simplicity, of perfect purity of diction:

Still is the toiling hand of Care;
 The panting herds repose:
Yet hark how through the peopled air
 The busy murmur glows!
The insect-youth are on the wing,
Eager to taste the honied spring,
And float amid the liquid noon:
Some lightly o'er the current skim,
Some show their gaily-gilded trim
 Quick-glancing to the sun.

'The language of the age is never the language of poetry', Gray declares, and certainly some of our great poets have created for themselves a diction which was never current, but it is equally true that some of the best English poetry has been written in a style which differs from the best spoken language only as the language of feeling will naturally diverge from the language of our less exalted moods. It was in the seventeenth-century poets that Wordsworth found the best corrective to the jargon of the later eighteenth-century poetry, descriptive and reflective, which he admired in his youth and imitated in his early poems; for as Coleridge pointed out, the style of the 'metaphysicals' 'is the reverse of that which distinguishes too many of our most recent versifiers; the one conveying the most fantastic thoughts in the most correct language, the other in the most fantastic language conveying the most trivial thoughts'.

But even the fantastic thoughts, the conceits of these courtly love poets and devout singers are not to be dismissed so lightly as a later, and still audible, criticism imagined. They played with thoughts, Sir Walter Scott complained, as the Elizabethans had played with words. But to play with thoughts it is necessary to think. 'To write on their plan', says Dr. Johnson, 'it was at least necessary to read and think. No man could be born a metaphysical poet, nor assume the dignity of a writer, by descriptions copied from descriptions, by imitations borrowed from imitations, by traditional imagery and hereditary similes, by readiness of rhyme and volubility of syllables.' Consider a poem, *The Repulse*, by a comparatively minor poet, Thomas Stanley. That is not a mere conceit. It is a new and felicitous rendering of a real and thrilling experience, the discovery that you might have fared worse in love than not to be loved, you might have been loved and then abandoned. Carew's *Ask me no more* is a coruscation of hyperboles, but

Now you have freely given me leave to love,
What will you do?

is a fresh and effective appeal to the heart of a woman. And this is what the metaphysicals are often doing in their unwearied play with conceits, delightfully naughty, extravagant, fantastic, frigid—they succeed in stumbling upon some conceit which reveals a fresh intuition into the heart, or states an old plea with new and prevailing force. And the divine poets express with the same blend of argument and imagination the deep and complex currents of religious feeling which were flowing in England throughout the century, institutional, theological, mystical, while in the metaphysical subtleties of conceit they found something that is more than conceit, symbols in which to express or adumbrate their apprehensions of the infinite.

The direct indebtedness of the courtly poets to Ben Jonson is probably, as Professor Gregory Smith has recently argued, small. But not only Herrick, metaphysical poets like Carew and Stanley and others owe much both of their turn of conceit and their care for form to Jonson's own models, the Latin lyrists,

Anacreon, the Greek Anthology, neo-Latin or Humanist poetry so rich in neat and pretty conceits. Some of them, as Crashaw and Stanley, and not only these, were familiar with Italian and Spanish poetry, Marino and Garcilasso and their elegantly elaborated confections. But their great master is Donne. If he taught them many heresies, he instilled into them at any rate the pure doctrine of the need of passion for a lover and a poet. What the young courtiers and university wits admired and reproduced in different degrees and fashions were his sensual audacity and the peculiar type of evolution which his poems accentuated, the strain of passionate paradoxical reasoning which knits the first line to the last and is perhaps a more intimate characteristic than even the far-fetched, fantastic comparisons. This intellectual, argumentative evolution had been of course a feature of the sonnet which might fancifully be called, with its double quatrain and sestet, the poetical analogy of the syllogism. But the movement of the sonnet is slow and meditative, a single thought expanded and articulated through the triple division, and the longer, decasyllabic line is the appropriate medium:

> Then hate me when thou wilt; if ever, now;
> Now while the world is bent my deeds to cross,
> Join with the spite of Fortune, make me bow,
> And do not drop in for an after-loss;
> Ah, do not when my heart hath scaped this sorrow,
> Come in the rearward of a conquer'd woe,
> Give not a windy night a rainy morrow,
> To linger out a purpos'd overthrow.
> If thou wilt leave me, do not leave me last
> When other petty griefs have done their spite,
> But in the onset come; so shall I taste
> At first the very worst of Fortune's might;
> And other strains of woe which now seem woe,
> Compared with loss of thee will not seem so.

What Donne had done was to quicken this movement, to intensify the strain of passionate ratiocination, passionate, paradoxical argument, and to carry it over from the sonnet to the song with its shorter lines, more winged and soaring movement, although the deeper strain of feeling which Donne shares with Shakespeare, and with Drayton at his best, made him partial to the longer line, at least as an element in his stanzas, and to longer and more intricate stanzas. Lightening both the feeling and the thought, the courtly poets simplified the verse, attaining some of their most wonderful effects in the common ballad measure [4, 3] or the longer [4, 4] measure in couplets or alternate rhymes. But the form and content are intimately associated. It is the elaboration of the paradoxical argument, the weight which the rhetoric lays on those syllables which fall under the metrical stress, that gives to these verses, or seems to give, their peculiar *élan*:

My love is of a birth as rare
  As 'tis for object strange and high;
It was begotten by Despair
  Upon Impossibility.

The audacious hyperboles and paradoxical turns of thought give breath to and take wings from the soaring rhythm.

It is needless here to dwell at length on the several poets from whom I have selected examples of love-song and complimentary verses. Their range is not wide—love, compliment, elegy, occasionally devotion. Herrick had to leave the court to learn the delights of nature and country superstitions. Lord Herbert of Cherbury, philosopher and coxcomb, was just the person to dilate on the Platonic theme of soul and body in the realm of love on which Donne occasionally descanted in half ironical fashion, Habington with tedious thin-blooded seriousness,

Cleveland and others with naughty irreverence. But Lord Herbert's *Ode*, which has been, like most of his poems, very badly edited, seems to me the finest thing inspired by Donne's *Ecstasy* and more characteristic of the romantic taste of the court of Charles. But the poetic ornament of that Court is Thomas Carew. This young careless liver was a careful artist with a deeper vein of thought and feeling in his temperament than a first reading suggests. His masque reveals the influence of Bruno. In Carew's poems and Vandyke's pictures the artistic taste of Charles's court is vividly reflected, a dignified voluptuousness, an exquisite elegance, if in some of the higher qualities of man and artist Carew is as inferior to Wyatt or Spenser as Vandyke is to Holbein. His *Ecstasy* is the most daring and poetically the happiest of the imitations of Donne's clever if outrageous elegies; Cartwright's *Song of Dalliance* its nearest rival. His letter to Aurelian Townshend on the death of the King of Sweden breathes the very enchanted air of Charles's court while the storm was brewing as yet unsuspected. The text of Richard Lovelace's *Lucasta* (1649) is frequently corrupt, and the majority of the poems are careless and extravagant, but the few good things are the finest expression of honour and chivalry in all the Cavalier poetry of the century, the only poems which suggest what 'Cavalier' came to mean when glorified by defeat. His *Grasshopper* has suffered a hard fate by textual corruption and from dismemberment in recent anthologies. Only the fantastic touch about 'green ice' ranks it as 'metaphysical', for it is in fact an experiment in the manner of the Horatian ode, not the heroic ode, but the lighter Epicurean, meditative strain of 'Solvitur acris hiems' and 'Vides ut alta stet nive candidum', description yielding abruptly to reflection. A slightly better text or a little more care on the poet's part would have made it perfect. The gayest of the group is Sir John Suckling, the writer of what should be called *vers de société*, a more careless but more fanciful Prior. His beautiful *Ballad on a Wedding* is a little outside the scope of this volume. Thomas Stanley, classical scholar, philosopher, translator, seems to me one of the happiest of recent recoveries, elegant, graceful, felicitous, and if at times a little flat and colourless, not always flat like the Catholic puritan William Habington.

But the strongest personality of all is Andrew Marvell. Apart from Milton he is the most interesting personality between Donne and Dryden, and at his very best a finer poet than either. Most of his descriptive poems lie a little outside my beat, though I have claimed *The Garden* as metaphysical,

> Annihilating all that's made
> To a green thought in a green shade,

and I might have claimed *The Nymph and the Faun* had space permitted. But his few love poems and his few devotional pieces are perfect exponents of all the 'metaphysical' qualities—passionate, paradoxical argument, touched with humour and learned imagery:

> As lines, so loves oblique, may well
>   Themselves in every angle greet:
> But ours so truly parallel,
>   Though infinite, can never meet;

and above all the sudden soar of passion in bold and felicitous image, in clangorous lines:

> But at my back I always hear
> Time's wingèd chariot hurrying near,
> And yonder all before us lie
> Deserts of vast eternity.
> Thy beauty shall no more be found;
> Nor in thy marble vault shall sound

My echoing song: then worms shall try
That long preserv'd virginity;
And your quaint honour turn to dust;
And into ashes all my lust.
The grave's a fine and private place,
But none I think do there embrace.

These lines seem to me the very roof and crown of the metaphysical love lyric, at once fantastic and passionate. Donne is weightier, more complex, more suggestive of subtle and profound reaches of feeling, but he has not one single passage of the same length that combines all the distinctive qualities of the kind, in thought, in phrasing, in feeling, in music; and Rochester's most passionate lines are essentially simpler, less metaphysical.

When wearied with a world of woe,

might have been written by Burns with some differences. The best things of Donne and Marvell could only have been composed—except, as an imitative *tour de force*, like Watson's

Bid me no more to other eyes—

in the seventeenth century. But in that century there were so many poets who could sing, at least occasionally, in the same strain. Of all those whom Professor Saintsbury's ardent and catholic but discriminating taste has collected there is none who has not written too much indifferent verse, but none who has not written one or two songs showing the same fine blend of passion and paradox and music. The 'metaphysicals' of the seventeenth century combined two things, both soon to pass away, the fantastic dialectics of mediaeval love poetry and the 'simple, sensuous' strain which they caught from the classics—soul and body lightly yoked and glad to run and soar together in the winged chariot of Pegasus. Modern love poetry has too often sacrificed both to sentiment.

III

English religious poetry after the Reformation was a long time in revealing a distinctive note of its own. Here as elsewhere, Protestant poetry took the shape mainly of Biblical paraphrases or dull moralizings less impressive and sombre than the *Poema Morale* of an earlier century. Sylvester's translation of Du Bartas's *Weeks and Days* eclipsed all previous efforts and appealed to Elizabethan taste by its conceits and aureate diction. Catholic poets, on the other hand, like Robert Southwell, learned from the Italians to write on religious themes in the antithetic, 'conceited', 'passionating' style of the love poets of the day. His *Tears of St. Peter*, if it is not demonstrably indebted to Tansillo's *Le Lagrime di San Pietro*, is composed in the same hectic strain and with a superabundance of the conceits and antitheses of that and other Italian religious poems of the sixteenth century:

> Launch forth, my soul, into a main of tears,
> Full-fraught with grief, the traffic of thy mind,
> Torn sails will serve, thoughts rent with guilty fears,
> Give care the stern, use sighs in lieu of wind:
> Remorse thy pilot; thy misdeeds thy card;
> Torment thy haven, shipwreck thy best reward.

His best poem, *The Burning Babe*, to have written which Jonson 'would have been content to destroy many of his', has the warmth and glow which we shall find again in the poetry of a Roman convert like Crashaw. It is in Donne's poems, *The Crosse, The Annuntiation and Passion, The Litanie*, that the Catholic tradition which survived in the Anglican Church becomes articulate in poetry; and in his sonnets and hymns that English religious poetry becomes for the first time intensely personal, the record of the experiences and aspirations, not of the Christian as such merely, but of one troubled and tormented soul. But the Catholic tradition in Donne was Roman rather than Anglican, or Anglican with something of a conscious effort; and Donne's passionate outpourings of penitence and longing lack one note of religious poetry which is audible in the songs of many less complex souls and less great poets, the note of attainment, of joy and peace. The waters have gone over him, the waters of fear and anguish, and it is only in his last hymns that he seems to descry across the agitation of the waves by which he is overwhelmed a light of hope and confidence:

> Swear by thyself that at my death thy Son
>   Shall shine as he shines now and heretofore;
> And having done that thou hast done,
>   I fear no more.

The poet in whom the English Church of Hooker and Laud, the Church of the *via media* in doctrine and ritual, found a voice of its own, was George Herbert, the son of Donne's friend Magdalen Herbert, and the younger brother of Lord Herbert of Cherbury. His volume *The Temple, Sacred Poems and Private Ejaculations, By Mr. George Herbert,* was printed at Cambridge in the year that a disorderly collection of the amorous, satirical, courtly and pious poems of the famous Dean of St. Paul's, who died in 1631, was shot from the press in London as *Poems, by J. D., with Elegies on the Author's Death.* As J. D. the author continued to figure on the title-page of each successive edition till that of 1669; nor were the additions made from time to time of a kind to diminish the complex, ambiguous impression which the volume must have produced on the minds of the admirers of the ascetic and eloquent Dean. There is no such record of a complex character and troubled progress in the poetry of Herbert. It was not, indeed, altogether without a struggle that Herbert bowed his neck to the collar, abandoned the ambitions and vanities of youth to become the pious rector of Bemerton. He knew, like Donne, in what light the ministry was regarded by the young courtiers whose days were spent

> In dressing, mistressing and compliment.

His ambitions had been courtly. He loved fine clothes. As Orator at Cambridge he showed himself an adept in learned and elegant flattery, and he hoped 'that, as his predecessors, he might in time attain the place of a Secretary of State'. When he resolved, after the death of 'his most obliging and powerful friends', to take Orders, he 'did acquaint a court-friend' with his resolution, 'who persuaded him to alter it, as too mean an employment, and too much below his birth, and the excellent abilities and endowments of his mind'. All this is clearly enough reflected in Herbert's poems, and I have endeavoured in my selection to emphasize the note of conflict, of personal experience, which troubles and gives life to poetry that might otherwise be too entirely doctrinal and didactic. But there is no evidence in Herbert's most agitated verses of the deeper scars, the profounder remorse which gives such a passionate, anguished *timbre* to the harsh but resonant harmonies of his older friend's *Divine Poems*:

> Despair behind, and death before doth cast
> Such terror, and my feeble flesh doth waste
> By sin in it, which it t'wards hell doth weigh.

Herbert knows the feeling of alienation from God; but he knows also that of reconcilement, the joy and peace of religion:

> You must sit down, says Love, and taste my meat:
> So I did sit and eat.

Herbert is too in full harmony with the Church of his country, could say, with Sir Thomas Browne, 'There is no Church whose every part so squares unto my Conscience; whose Articles, Constitutions and Customs, seem so consonant unto reason, and as it were framed to my particular Devotion, as this whereof I hold my Belief, the Church of England':

Beauty in thee takes up her place,
And dates her letters from thy face,
When she doth write.

A fine aspect in fit array,
Neither too mean, nor yet too gay,
Shows who is best.

. . . .

But, dearest Mother, (what those misse)
The mean, thy praise and glory is,
And long may be.

Blessed be God, whose love it was
To double moat thee with his grace,
And none but thee.

It was from Donne that Herbert learned the 'metaphysical' manner. He has none of Donne's daring applications of scholastic doctrines. Herbert's interest in theology is not metaphysical but practical and devotional, the doctrines of his Church—the Incarnation, Passion, Resurrection, Trinity, Baptism—as these are reflected in the festivals, fabric, and order of the Church and are capable of appeal to the heart. But Herbert's central theme is the psychology of his religious experiences. He transferred to religious poetry the subtler analysis and record of moods which had been Donne's great contribution to love poetry. The metaphysical taste in conceit, too, ingenious, erudite, and indiscriminate, not confining itself to the conventionally picturesque and poetic, appealed to his acute, if not profound mind, and to the Christian temper which rejected nothing as common and unclean. He would speak of sacred things in the simplest language and with the aid of the homeliest comparisons:

> Both heav'n and earth
> Paid me my wages in a world of mirth.

Prayer is:

> Heaven in ordinary, man well drest,
> The milky way, the bird of Paradise.

Divine grace in the Sacramental Elements:

> Knoweth the ready way,
> And hath the privy key
> Op'ning the soul's most subtle rooms;
> While those, to spirits refin'd, at door attend
> Dispatches from their friend.

Night is God's 'ebony box' in which:

> Thou dost inclose us till the day
> Put our amendment in our way,
> And give new wheels to our disorder'd clocks.

> Christ left his grave-clothes that we might, when grief
> Draws tears or blood, not want an handkerchief.

These are the 'mean' similes which in Dr. Johnson's view were fatal to poetic effect even in Shakespeare. We have learned not to be so fastidious, yet when they are not purified by the passionate heat of the poet's dramatic imagination the effect is a little stuffy, for the analogies and symbols are more fanciful or traditional than natural and imaginative. Herbert's nature is generally 'metaphysical',—'the busy orange-tree', the rose that purges, the 'sweet spring' which is 'a box where sweets compacted lie'. It is at rare moments that feeling and natural image are imaginatively and completely merged in one another:

And now in age I bud again,
After so many deaths I live and write;
I once more smell the dew and rain,
And relish versing: O my only light,
It cannot be
That I am he
On whom thy tempests fell all night.

But if not a greatly imaginative, Herbert is a sincere and sensitive poet, and an accomplished artist elaborating his argumentative strain or little allegories and conceits with felicitous completeness, and managing his variously patterned stanzas—even the symbolic wings and altars and priestly bells, the three or seven-lined stanzas of his poems on the Trinity and Sunday—with a finished and delicate harmony. *The Temple* breathes the spirit of the Anglican Church at its best, primitive and modest; and also of one troubled and delicate soul seeking and finding peace.

Herbert's influence is discernible in the religious verse of all the minor Anglican poets of the century, but his two greatest followers were poets of a temper different from his own. Henry Vaughan had written verses of the fashionable kind—I have included one mild if elegant love-poem—before the influence of Herbert converted his pen to the service of Heaven; but all his *poetry* is religious. In *Silex Scintillans* he often imitates his predecessor in name and choice of theme, but his best work is of another kind. The difference between Herbert and Vaughan, at his best, is the difference on which Coleridge and Wordsworth dilated between fancy and imagination, between the sensitive and happy discovery of analogies and the imaginative apprehension of emotional identity in diverse experiences, which is the poet's counterpart to the scientific discovery of a common law controlling the most divergent phenomena. Herbert's 'sweet day, so cool, so calm, so bright' is a delightful play of tender fancy. Vaughan's greatest verses reveal a profounder intuition, as when Night is:

God's silent, searching flight;
When my Lord's head is fill'd with dew, and all
His locks are wet with the clear drops of night;
His still, soft call;
His knocking-time; the soul's dumb watch
When spirits their fair kindred catch.

Vaughan is a less effective preacher, a far less neat and finished artist than Herbert. His temper is more that of the mystic. The sense of guilt which troubles Donne, of sin which is the great alienator of man's soul from God in Herbert's poems, is less acute with Vaughan, or is merged in a wider consciousness of separation, a veil between the human soul and that Heaven which is its true home. His soul is ever questing, back to the days of his own youth, or to the youth of the world, or to the days of Christ's sojourn on earth, when God and man were in more intimate contact:

In Abraham's tent the winged guests
—O how familiar then was heaven!—
Eat, drink, discourse, sit down and rest,
Until the cool and shady even;

or else he yearns for the final reconciliation beyond the grave:

Where no rude shade or night
Shall dare approach us; we shall there no more
Watch stars or pore
Through melancholy clouds, and say,
'Would it were Day!'
One everlasting Sabbath there shall run
Without succession, and without a sun.

To this mystical mood Nature reveals herself, not as a museum of spiritual analogies, a garden of religious simples, but as a creature simpler than man, yet, in virtue of its simplicity and innocence, in closer harmony with God. 'Etenim res creatae exserto capite observantes exspectant revelationem filiorum Dei.' At brief moments Vaughan writes of nature and childhood as Wordsworth and Blake were to write, but generally with the addition of some little pietistic tag which betrays his century. It is indeed only in short passages that Vaughan achieves adequate imaginative vision and utterance, but the spirit of these passages is diffused through his religious verse, more quietistic, less practical, in spirit than Herbert's.

Vaughan's quietist and mystical, Herbert's restrained and ordered, temper and poetry are equally remote from the radiant spirit of Richard Crashaw. Herbert's conceits are quaint or homely analogies, Vaughan's are the blots of a fashion on a style naturally pure and simple. Crashaw's long odes give the impression at first reading of soaring rockets scattering balls of coloured fire, the 'happy fireworks' to which he compares St. Teresa's writings. His conceits are more after the confectionery manner of the Italians than the scholastic or homely manner of the followers of Donne. Neither spiritual conflict controlled and directed by Christian inhibitions and aspirations, nor mystical yearning for a closer communion with the divine, is the burden of his religious song, but love, tenderness, and joy. In Crashaw's poetry, as in the later poetry of the Dutch Vondel, a note is heard which is struck for the first time in the seventeenth century, the accent of the convert to Romanism, the joy of the troubled soul who has found rest and a full expansion of heart in the rediscovery of a faith and ritual and order which give entire satisfaction to the imagination and affections. And that is not quite all. The Catholic poet is set free from the painful diagnosis of his own emotions and spiritual condition which so preoccupies the Anglican Herbert:

How should I praise thee, Lord! how should my rhymes
Gladly engrave thy name in steel,
If what my soul doth feel sometimes
My soul might ever feel!

Although there were some forty heav'ns or more,
Sometimes I peer above them all;
Sometimes I hardly reach a score,
Sometimes to hell I fall.

The Catholic poet loses this anxious sense of his own moods in the consciousness of the *opus operatum* calling on him only for faith and thankfulness and adoration. It is this *opus operatum* in one or other of its aspects or symbols, the Cross, the name of Christ, the Incarnation, the Eucharist, the life of the saint or death of the martyr, which is the theme of all Crashaw's ardent and coloured, sensuous and conceited odes, composed in irregular rhythms which rise and fall like a sparkling fountain. All other moods are merged in faith and love:

Faith can believe
As fast as love new laws can give.
Faith is my force. Faith strength affords
To keep pace with those powerful words.
And words more sure, more sweet than they
Love could not think, truth could not say.

Crashaw's poetry has a limited compass of moods, but it has two of the supreme qualities of great lyric poetry, poetry such as that of Shelley and Swinburne, ardour and music.

Of the other poets from whose work I have selected not much need be said. Quarles hardly belongs to the 'metaphysical' tradition. In his paraphrases of Scripture he continues the

Elizabethan fashion of Drayton and the later Giles Fletcher, but in the *Emblemes* [1635, 1639, 1643] he is a religious lyrist of real if unequal power, with the taste for quaint and homely analogy of Herbert. I have felt no disposition to cut and carve the sincere and ardent poems selected to represent his sense of alienation and reconcilement. To include Milton's *Hymn* in an anthology of metaphysical poems will seem less warrantable, for Milton is not enamoured of the quaint, the homely, or the too ratiocinative evolution, though he was also an erudite poet. Yet it would be to fail in literary perspective not to recognize that in this poem Milton wrote in a manner he was not to use again, that his models here are Italian rather than classical (the poem may owe something to Tasso's *Canzone sopra la Cappella del Presepio*), that the verses are a sequence of poetical and delightful conceits, some of which, as that of the blushing earth and the snow, or the

Glimmering Orbs 'that' glow,
Until their Lord himself bespake, and bid them go,

are not very remote from the blushing dagger on which Boileau commented. Milton's style was to become more uniformly classical, but with the conceits departed alas! also the tenderness of spirit that gives to this early poem an ineffable charm.

Milton's young friend Andrew Marvell imbibed no more of Milton's classical inspiration than his graceless nephews and pupils, the Phillipses. In his religious as in his amorous and descriptive verses he is a 'metaphysical' dallying with poetic conceits in pure and natural English. But the temper of these few poems is of the finest that the Puritan movement begot, as devoted to the 'restrictive virtues' as Milton's, with less of polemical narrowness and arrogance; the temper of one in the world yet not of the world, recognizing and loyal to a scale of values that is not the world's:

> Earth cannot show so brave a sight
> As when a single soul does fence
> The batteries of alluring sense,
> And heaven views it with delight.

In no poetry more than the religious did the English genius in the seventeenth century declare its strong individuality, its power of reacting on the traditions and fashions which, in the Elizabethan age, had flowed in upon it from the Latin countries of Europe. There are individual poets who have risen to greater heights of religious and mystical feeling—some of the mediaeval hymn-writers, Dante, perhaps John of the Cross—but no country or century has produced a more individual or varied devout poetry, resting on the fundamental religious experience of alienation from and reconciliation to God, complicated by ecclesiastical and individual varieties of temperament and interpretation, than the country and century of Giles Fletcher and John Donne, Herbert and Vaughan, and Traherne and Crashaw, of John Milton, to say nothing of great poet-preachers like Donne and Taylor, or the allegory of Bunyan and the musings of Sir Thomas Brown.

IV

When Dryden and his generation passed judgement, not merely on the conceits, but on the form of the earlier poetry, what they had in view was especially their use of the decasyllabic couplet in eulogistic, elegiac, and satiric and narrative verses. 'All of them were thus far of Eugenius his opinion that the sweetness of English verse was never understood or practised by our fathers . . . and every one was willing to acknowledge how much our poesy is improved by the happiness of some writers yet living, who first taught us to mould our thoughts into easy and significant words, to retrench the superfluities of expression, and to make our rhyme so properly a part of the verse, that it should never mislead the sense, but itself be led and governed by it.' 'Donne alone', Dryden tells the Earl of Dorset, 'of all our countrymen had your talent: but was not happy enough to arrive at your versification; and were he translated into numbers and English, he would yet be wanting in the dignity of expression.' Sweetness and strength of versification, dignity of expression—these were the qualities which Dryden and his generation believed they had conferred upon English poetry. 'There was before the time of Dryden no poetical diction, no system of words at once refined from the grossness of domestic use, and free from the harshness of terms appropriated to particular arts. . . . Those happy combinations of words which distinguish poetry from prose had been rarely attempted; we had few elegances or flowers of speech, the roses had not yet been plucked from the brambles, or different colours had not been joined to enliven one another.' Johnson is amplifying and emphasizing Dryden's 'dignity of expression', and it is well to remember that Scott at the beginning of the next century is still of the same opinion. It is also worth remembering, in order to see a critical period of our poetical history in a true perspective, that Milton fully shared Dryden's opinion of the poetry of his time, though he had a different conception of how poetic diction and verse should be reformed. He, too, one may gather from his practice and from occasional references, disapproved the want of selection in the 'metaphysicals'' diction, and created for himself a poetic idiom far removed from current speech. His fine and highly trained ear disliked the frequent harshness of their versification, their indifference to the well-ordered melody of vowel and consonant, the grating, 'scrannel pipe' concatenations which he notes so scornfully in the verse of Bishop Hall:

> 'Teach each hollow grove to sound his love
> Wearying echo with one changeless word.

And so he well might, and all his auditory besides, with his "teach each"' (*An Apology for Smectymnuus*). But the flowers which Milton cultivated are not those of Dryden, nor was his ear satisfied with the ring of the couplet. He must have disliked as much as Dryden the breathless, headlong overflow of *Pharonnida* (if he ever read it), the harsh and abrupt crossing of the rhythmical by the rhetorical pattern of Donne's *Satires*, but he knew that the secret of harmonious verse lay in this subtle crossing and blending of the patterns, 'apt numbers, fit quantity of syllables, and the sense variously drawn out from one verse into another'. Spenser was Milton's poetic father, and his poetic diction and elaborately varied harmony are a development of Spenser's art by one who has absorbed more completely the spirit, understood more perfectly the art, of Virgil and the Greeks, who has taken Virgil and Homer for his teachers rather than Ariosto and Tasso. Dryden's reform was due to no such adherence to an older and more purely poetic tradition though he knew and admired the ancients. His development was on the line of Donne and the metaphysicals, their assimilation of poetic idiom and rhythm to that of the spoken language, but the talk of which Dryden's poetry is an idealization is more choice and select, less natural and fanciful, and rises more frequently to the level of oratory. Like other reforms, Dryden's was in great measure a change of fashion. Men's minds and ears were disposed to welcome a new tone and tune, a new accent, neither that of high song,

> passionate thoughts
> To their own music chanted,

nor of easy, careless, but often delightful talk and song blended, which is the tone of the metaphysical lyric, but the accent of the orator, the political orator of a constitutional country.

It was in satire, the Satires of Hall, Marston, and Donne—especially the last—that the 'unscrewing' of the decasyllabic couplet began, in part as a deliberate effort to reproduce the colloquial ease of Horace's, the harshness of Persius's satiric style and verse. The fashion quickly spread to narrative, eulogistic, elegiac, and reflective poetry, and like other fashions—*vers libre* for example—was welcomed by many who found in it an easier *gradus ad Parnassum*, a useful discovery when every one had at times to pen a compliment to friend or patron.

After Spenser Elizabethan narrative poetry suffered almost without exception from the 'uncontented care to write better than one could', the sacrifice of story and character to the elaboration of sentimental and descriptive rhetoric. Shakespeare's *Venus and Adonis* and *Rape of Lucrece* are no exception to this failure to secure that perfect balance of narrative, dramatic and poetic interest, which makes Chaucer's tales unsurpassed models in their kind. The 'metaphysical' fashion changed merely the character of the rhetoric, shifting the weight from diction and verse to wit, to *διάνοια*. One can study the result in Davenant's *Gondibert* and Cowley's *Davideis*, where the dramatic thread of story is almost lost to sight in the embroidery of comment and 'witty' simile:

> Oswald in wars was worthily renowned;
>   Though gay in Courts, coarsely in Camps could live;
> Judg'd danger soon, and first was in it found;
>   Could toil to gain what he with ease did give.
>
> Yet toils and dangers through ambition lov'd;
>   Which does in war the name of Virtue own;
> But quits that name when from the war remov'd,
>   As Rivers theirs when from their Channels gone.

The most readable—if with somewhat of a wrestle—is Chamberlayne's *Pharonnida.* The story is compounded of the tedious elements of Greek romance—shepherds and courts and loves and rapes and wars—and no one can take the smallest interest in the characters. The verse is breathless and the style obscure, as that of Mr. Doughty is, because the writer uses the English language as if he had found it lying about and was free of it without regard to any tradition of idiom or structure. Still Chamberlayne does realize the scenes which he describes and decorates with all the arabesques of a fantastic and bewildering yet poetic wit:

> The Spring did, when
> The princess first did with her pleasure grace
> This house of pleasure, with soft arms embrace
> The Earth—his lovely mistress—clad in all
> The painted robes the morning's dew let fall
> Upon her virgin bosom; the soft breath
> Of Zephyrus sung calm anthems at the death
> Of palsy-shaken Winter, whose large grave,
> The earth, whilst they in fruitful tears did lave,
> Their pious grief turned into smiles, they throw
> Over the hearse a veil of flowers; the low
> And pregnant valleys swelled with fruit, whilst Heaven
> Smiled on each blessing its fair hand had given.

But the peculiar territory of the metaphysical poets, outside love-song and devout verse, was eulogy and elegy. They were pedants but also courtiers abounding in compliments to royal and noble patrons and friends and fellow poets. Here again Donne is the great exemplar of erudite and transcendental, subtle and seraphic compliments to noble and benevolent countesses. One may doubt whether the thing ought to be done at all. but there can be no doubt that Donne does it well, and no one was better aware of the fact than Dryden, whose eulogies, whether in verse or in prose, as the dedication of the *State of Innocence* to Mary of Modena, are in the same seraphic vein and indeed contain lines that are boldly 'lifted' from Donne. They are not vivid by the accumulation of concrete details, though there are some not easily to be surpassed, as Ben Jonson's favourite lines:

> No need of lanterns, and in one place lay
> Feathers and dust, to-day and yesterday.

But the most vivid impressions are secured not by objective detail, but by the suggestion of their effect upon the mind. The nervous effect of storm and calm is conveyed by Donne's conceits and hyperboles in a way that is not only vivid but intense.

One cannot say much for the metaphysical eulogies of Donne's imitators. Even Professor Saintsbury has omitted many of them from his collection of the other poems by their authors, as Godolphin's lines on Donne and on Sandys's version of the Psalms, which are by no means the worst of their kind. He has, on the other hand, included one, Cleveland's on Edward King, some lines of which might be quoted to illustrate the extravagances of the fashion:

> I like not tears in tune, nor do I prize
> His artificial grief who scans his eyes.
> Mine weep down pious beads, but why should I
> Confine them to the Muses' rosary?
> I am no poet here; my pen's the spout
> Where the rain-water of mine eyes run out
> In pity of that name, whose fate we see
> Thus copied out in grief's hydrography.
> The Muses are not mermaids, though upon
> His death the ocean might turn Helicon.

. . . .

When we have filled the roundlets of our eyes
We'll issue 't forth and vent such elegies
As that our tears shall seem the Irish Seas,
We floating islands, living Hebrides.

The last word recalls the great poem which appeared along with it:

Where ere thy bones are hurl'd,
Whether beyond the stormy Hebrides,
Where thou perhaps under the whelming tide
Visit'st the bottom of the monstrous world.

Cleveland is not much worse than Joseph Beaumont on the same subject, and neither is quite so offensive as Francis Beaumont in his lines on the death of Mrs. Markham:

As unthrifts grieve in straw for their pawned beds,
As women weep for their lost maidenheads
(When both are without hope of remedy),
Such an untimely grief have I for thee.

It would be difficult to imagine anything in worse taste, yet, from the frequency with which the poem recurs in manuscript collections, it was apparently admired as a flight of 'wit'. There are better elegies than these, as Herrick's and Earle's and Stanley's on Beaumont and Fletcher, Cleveland's (if it be his) on Jonson, Carew's noble lines on Donne, but in proportion as they become readable they cease to be metaphysical. Donne's *a priori* transcendentalism few or none were able to recapture. Their attempts to rise meet the fate of Icarus. The lesser metaphysical poets are most happy and most poetical when their theme is not this or that individual but death in general. Love and death are the foci round which they moved in eccentric cycles and epicycles. Their mood is not the sombre mediaeval horror of 'Earth upon earth', nor the blended horror and fascination of Donne's elegies, or the more magnificent prose of his sermons. They dwell less in the Charnel House. Their strain is one of pensive reflection on the fleetingness of life, relieved by Christian resignation and hope:

> Like as the damask rose you see,
> Or like the blossom on the tree,
> Or like the dainty flower in May,
> Or like the morning of the day,
> Or like the sun, or like the shade,
> Or like the gourd which Jonas had—
> Even such is man: whose thread is spun,
> Drawn out and cut and so is done.
>
> If none can scape Death's dreadful dart,
> If rich and poor his beck obey,
> If strong, if wise, if all do smart,
> Then I to scape shall have no way.
> O grant me grace, O God, that I
> My life may mend since I must die.

In Abraham Cowley 'metaphysical' poetry produced its last considerable representative, and a careful study of his poetry reveals clearly what was the fate which overtook it. His wit is far less bizarre and extravagant than much in Donne, to say nothing of Cleveland and Benlowes. But the central heat has died down. Less extravagant, his wit is also less passionate and imaginative. The long wrestle between reason and the imagination has ended in the victory of reason, good sense. The subtleties of the schoolmen have for Cowley none of the significance and interest they possessed for Donne:

> So did this noble Empire wast,
> Sunk by degrees from glories past,
> And in the School-men's hands it perished quite at last.
> Then nought but words it grew,
> And those all barbarous too.
> It perish't and it vanisht there,
> The life and soul breath'd out, became but empty air.

The influence of the new philosophy simplified with such dogmatic simplicity by Hobbes has touched him,—atoms and determinism, witness the ode *To Mr. Hobbes* and the half-playful, charming *Destinie*; and though that philosophy might appeal to the imagination, the intellectual imagination, by its apparent simplicity and coherency, it could make no such appeal to the spiritual nature as the older, which had its roots in the heart and conscience, which had endeavoured to construct a view of things which should include, which indeed made central, the requirements and values of the human soul. Cowley is not wanting in feeling any more than in fancy, witness his poem *On the Death of Mr. William Hervey*, and he was a Christian, but neither his affections nor his devotion expressed themselves imaginatively as these feelings did in Donne's most sombre or bizarre verses or those of his spiritual followers; his wit is not the reflection of a sombre or bizarre, a passionately coloured or mystically tinted conception of life and love and death. The fashion of 'metaphysical' wit remains in Cowley's poems when the spirit that gave it colour and music is gone. Yet Cowley's poetry is not merely frigid and fantastic. The mind and temper which his delightful essays, and the poems which accompany them, express has its own real charm—a mind of shy sensitiveness and clear good sense. It was by a natural affinity that Cowley's poetry appealed to Cowper. But wit which is not passionate and imaginative must appeal in some other way, and in Dryden it began to do so by growing eloquent. The interest shifted from thought to form, the expression not the novelty of the thought, wit polished and refined as an instrument of satire and compliment and declamation on themes of common interest. Dryden and Pope brought our witty poetry to a brilliant close. They are the last great poets of an age of intense intellectual activity and controversy, theological, metaphysical, political. 'The present age is a little too warlike', Atterbury thought, for blank verse and a great poem. With the peace of the Augustans the mood changed, and poetry, ceasing to be witty, became sentimental; but great poetry is always metaphysical, born of men's passionate thinking about life and love and death.

I have closed my selections from seventeenth-century poetry not with Cowley or Dryden, but with Butler as a reminder of the full significance of the word 'metaphysical', which has a wider connotation than poetry. The century was metaphysical, and the great civil war was a metaphysical war. So many constitutional developments have been the ultimate consequence of the movement which the war began that it has obscured to our eyes the issue as it appeared to the combatants. To them the main issue was not constitutional. Pym and Parliament were more indifferent to the constitution than Charles and Clarendon. Cromwell's army was not inspired by any passion for the constitution; it fought to found the Kingdom of the Saints. Butler's *Hudibras* is a savage record of what the human spirit had suffered under the tyranny of metaphysical saints.

∵ My selection, like every selection, is a compromise between what one would like to give and what space permits. Inevitably, too, I have omitted one or two poems which on second thoughts I might prefer to some of those included. I regret especially that 'wonderful piece of word-craft', *Musics Duel.* Such as it is, my selection owes more than I can easily define to the suggestions, encouragement, advice—even when we occasionally differed in opinion—and patient scrutiny of the general editor, Mr. David Nichol Smith.

P O E M S

Love Poems

Divine Poems

Miscellanies

LOVE POEMS.

The good-morrow.

I Wonder by my troth, what thou, and I
Did, till we lov'd? were we not wean'd till then?
But suck'd on countrey pleasures, childishly?
Or snorted we in the seaven sleepers den?
T'was so; But this, all pleasures fancies bee.
If ever any beauty I did see,
Which I desir'd, and got, t'was but a dreame of thee.

And now good morrow to our waking soules,
Which watch not one another out of feare;
For love, all love of other sights controules,
And makes one little roome, an every where.
Let sea-discoverers to new worlds have gone,
Let Maps to other, worlds on worlds have showne,
Let us possesse one world, each hath one, and is one.

My face in thine eye, thine in mine appeares,
And true plaine hearts doe in the faces rest,
Where can we finde two better hemispheares
Without sharpe North, without declining West?
What ever dyes, was not mixt equally;
If our two loves be one, or, thou and I
Love so alike, that none doe slacken, none can die.

John Donne.

Song.

GOe, and catche a falling starre,
  Get with child a mandrake roote,
Tell me, where all past yeares are,
  Or who cleft the Divels foot,
Teach me to heare Mermaides singing,
  Or to keep off envies stinging,
    And finde
    What winde
Serves to advance an honest minde.

If thou beest borne to strange sights,
  Things invisible to see,
Ride ten thousand daies and nights,
  Till age snow white haires on thee,
Thou, when thou retorn'st, wilt tell mee
All strange wonders that befell thee,
    And sweare
    No where
Lives a woman true, and faire.

If thou findst one, let mee know,
  Such a Pilgrimage were sweet;
Yet doe not, I would not goe,
  Though at next doore wee might meet,
Though shee were true, when you met her,
And last, till you write your letter,
    Yet shee
    Will bee
False, ere I come, to two, or three.

John Donne.

The Sunne Rising.

BUsie old foole, unruly Sunne,
Why dost thou thus,
Through windowes, and through curtaines call on us?
Must to thy motions lovers seasons run?
Sawcy pedantique wretch, goe chide
Late schoole boyes, and sowre prentices,
Goe tell Court-huntsmen, that the King will ride,
Call countrey ants to harvest offices;
Love, all alike, no season knowes, nor clyme,
Nor houres, dayes, moneths, which are the rags of time.

Thy beames, so reverend, and strong
Why shouldst thou thinke?
I could eclipse and cloud them with a winke,
But that I would not lose her sight so long:
If her eyes have not blinded thine,
Looke, and to morrow late, tell mee,
Whether both the'India's of spice and Myne
Be where thou leftst them, or lie here with mee.
Aske for those Kings whom thou saw'st yesterday,
And thou shalt heare, All here in one bed lay.

She'is all States, and all Princes, I,
Nothing else is.
Princes doe but play us; compar'd to this,
All honor's mimique; All wealth alchimie.
Thou sunne art halfe as happy'as wee,
In that the world's contracted thus;

Thine age askes ease, and since thy duties bee
To warme the world, that's done in warming us.
Shine here to us, and thou art every where ;
This bed thy center is, these walls, thy spheare.

John Donne.

Lovers infinitenesse.

IF yet I have not all thy love,
Deare, I shall never have it all,
I cannot breath one other sigh, to move,
Nor can intreat one other teare to fall,
And all my treasure, which should purchase thee,
Sighs, teares, and oathes, and letters I have spent.
Yet no more can be due to mee,
Then at the bargaine made was ment,
If then thy gift of love were partiall,
That some to mee, some should to others fall,
Deare, I shall never have Thee All.

Or if then thou gavest mee all,
All was but All, which thou hadst then ;
But if in thy heart, since, there be or shall,
New love created bee, by other men,
Which have their stocks intire, and can in teares,
In sighs, in oathes, and letters outbid mee,
This new love may beget new feares,
For, this love was not vowed by thee.
And yet it was, thy gift being generall,
The ground, thy heart is mine, what ever shall
Grow there, deare, I should have it all.

Yet I would not have all yet,
Hee that hath all can have no more,
And since my love doth every day admit
New growth, thou shouldst have new rewards in store;
Thou canst not every day give me thy heart,
If thou canst give it, then thou never gavest it:
Loves riddles are, that though thy heart depart,
It stayes at home, and thou with losing savest it:
But wee will have a way more liberall,
Then changing hearts, to joyne them, so wee shall
Be one, and one anothers All.

John Donne.

Song.

SWeetest love, I do not goe,
For wearinesse of thee,
Nor in hope the world can show
A fitter Love for mee;
But since that I
Must dye at last, 'tis best,
To use my selfe in jest
Thus by fain'd deaths to dye;

Yesternight the Sunne went hence,
And yet is here to day,
He hath no desire nor sense,
Nor halfe so short a way:
Then feare not mee,
But beleeve that I shall make
Speedier journeyes, since I take
More wings and spurres then hee.

O how feeble is mans power,
That if good fortune fall,
Cannot adde another houre,
Nor a lost houre recall!
But come bad chance,
And wee joyne to'it our strength,
And wee teach it art and length,
It selfe o'r us to advance.

When thou sigh'st, thou sigh'st not winde,
But sigh'st my soule away,
When thou weep'st, unkindly kinde,
My lifes blood doth decay.
It cannot bee
That thou lov'st mee, as thou say'st,
If in thine my life thou waste,
Thou art the best of mee.

Let not thy divining heart
Forethinke me any ill,
Destiny may take thy part,
And may thy feares fulfill;
But thinke that wee
Are but turn'd aside to sleepe;
They who one another keepe
Alive, ne'r parted bee.

John Donne.

Aire and Angels.

TWice or thrice had I loved thee,
Before I knew thy face or name;
So in a voice, so in a shapelesse flame,
Angells affect us oft, and worship'd bee;
Still when, to where thou wert, I came,
Some lovely glorious nothing I did see.
But since my soule, whose child love is,
Takes limmes of flesh, and else could nothing doe,
More subtile then the parent is,
Love must not be, but take a body too,
And therefore what thou wert, and who,
I bid Love aske, and now
That it assume thy body, I allow,
And fixe it selfe in thy lip, eye, and brow.

Whilst thus to ballast love, I thought,
And so more steddily to have gone,
With wares which would sinke admiration,
I saw, I had loves pinnace overfraught,
Ev'ry thy haire for love to worke upon
Is much too much, some fitter must be sought;
For, nor in nothing, nor in things
Extreme, and scatt'ring bright, can love inhere;
Then as an Angell, face, and wings
Of aire, not pure as it, yet pure doth weare,
So thy love may be my loves spheare;
Just such disparitie
As is twixt Aire and Angells puritie,
'Twixt womens love, and mens will ever bee.

John Donne.

The Anniversarie.

ALL Kings, and all their favorites,
  All glory of honors, beauties, wits,
The Sun it selfe, which makes times, as they passe,
Is elder by a yeare, now, then it was
When thou and I first one another saw:
All other things, to their destruction draw,
  Only our love hath no decay;
This, no to morrow hath, nor yesterday,
Running it never runs from us away,
But truly keepes his first, last, everlasting day.

  Two graves must hide thine and my coarse,
  If one might, death were no divorce.
Alas, as well as other Princes, wee,
(Who Prince enough in one another bee,)
Must leave at last in death, these eyes, and eares,
Oft fed with true oathes, and with sweet salt teares;
  But soules where nothing dwells but love
(All other thoughts being inmates) then shall prove
This, or a love increased there above,
When bodies to their graves, soules from their graves remove.

  And then wee shall be throughly blest,
  But wee no more, then all the rest;
Here upon earth, we'are Kings, and none but wee
Can be such Kings, nor of such subjects bee.
Who is so safe as wee? where none can doe
Treason to us, except one of us two.
  True and false feares let us refraine,
Let us love nobly, and live, and adde againe
Yeares and yeares unto yeares, till we attaine
To write threescore: this is the second of our raigne.

John Donne.

Twicknam garden.

BLasted with sighs, and surrounded with teares,
Hither I come to seeke the spring,
And at mine eyes, and at mine eares,
Receive such balmes, as else cure every thing;
But O, selfe traytor, I do bring
The spider love, which transubstantiates all,
And can convert Manna to gall,
And that this place may thoroughly be thought
True Paradise, I have the serpent brought.

'Twere wholsomer for mee, that winter did
Benight the glory of this place,
And that a grave frost did forbid
These trees to laugh, and mocke mee to my face;
But that I may not this disgrace
Indure, nor yet leave loving, Love let mee
Some senslesse peece of this place bee;
Make me a mandrake, so I may groane here,
Or a stone fountaine weeping out my yeare.

Hither with christall vyals, lovers come,
And take my teares, which are loves wine,
And try your mistresse Teares at home,
For all are false, that tast not just like mine;
Alas, hearts do not in eyes shine,
Nor can you more judge womans thoughts by teares,
Then by her shadow, what she weares.
O perverse sexe, where none is true but shee,
Who's therefore true, because her truth kills mee.

John Donne.

The Dreame.

DEare love, for nothing lesse then thee
Would I have broke this happy dreame,
It was a theame
For reason, much too strong for phantasie,
Therefore thou wakd'st me wisely; yet
My Dreame thou brok'st not, but continued'st it,
Thou art so truth, that thoughts of thee suffice,
To make dreames truths; and fables histories;
Enter these armes, for since thou thoughtst it best,
Not to dreame all my dreame, let's act the rest.

As lightning, or a Tapers light,
Thine eyes, and not thy noise wak'd mee;
Yet I thought thee
(For thou lovest truth) an Angell, at first sight,
But when I saw thou sawest my heart,
And knew'st my thoughts, beyond an Angels art,
When thou knew'st what I dreamt, when thou knew'st when
Excesse of joy would wake me, and cam'st then,
I must confesse, it could not chuse but bee
Prophane, to thinke thee any thing but thee.

Comming and staying show'd thee, thee,
But rising makes me doubt, that now,
Thou art not thou.
That love is weake, where feare's as strong as hee;
'Tis not all spirit, pure, and brave,
If mixture it of *Feare*, *Shame*, *Honor*, have.
Perchance as torches which must ready bee,
Men light and put out, so thou deal'st with mee,
Thou cam'st to kindle, goest to come; Then I
Will dreame that hope againe, but else would die.

John Donne.

A Valediction: of weeping.

LEt me powre forth
My teares before thy face, whil'st I stay here,
For thy face coines them, and thy stampe they beare,
And by this Mintage they are something worth,
For thus they bee
Pregnant of thee;
Fruits of much griefe they are, emblemes of more,
When a teare falls, that thou falst which it bore,
So thou and I are nothing then, when on a divers shore.

On a round ball
A workeman that hath copies by, can lay
An Europe, Afrique, and an Asia,
And quickly make that, which was nothing, *All*,
So doth each teare,
Which thee doth weare,
A globe, yea world by that impression grow,
Till thy teares mixt with mine doe overflow
This world, by waters sent from thee, my heaven dissolved so.

O more then Moone,
Draw not up seas to drowne me in thy spheare,
Weepe me not dead, in thine armes, but forbeare
To teach the sea, what it may doe too soone;
Let not the winde
Example finde,
To doe me more harme, then it purposeth;
Since thou and I sigh one anothers breath,
Who e'r sighes most, is cruellest, and hasts the others death.

John Donne.

The Message.

SEnd home my long strayd eyes to mee,
Which (Oh) too long have dwelt on thee;
Yet since there they have learn'd such ill,
Such forc'd fashions,
And false passions,
That they be
Made by thee
Fit for no good sight, keep them still.

Send home my harmlesse heart againe,
Which no unworthy thought could staine;
But if it be taught by thine
To make jestings
Of protestings,
And crosse both
Word and oath,
Keepe it, for then 'tis none of mine.

Yet send me back my heart and eyes,
That I may know, and see thy lyes,
And may laugh and joy, when thou
Art in anguish
And dost languish
For some one
That will none,
Or prove as false as thou art now.

John Donne.

A nocturnall upon S. Lucies *day,*
Being the shortest day.

TIs the yeares midnight, and it is the dayes,
Lucies, who scarce seaven houres herself unmaskes,
The Sunne is spent, and now his flasks
Send forth light squibs, no constant rayes;
The worlds whole sap is sunke:
The generall balme th'hydroptique earth hath drunk,
Whither, as to the beds-feet, life is shrunke,
Dead and enterr'd; yet all these seeme to laugh,
Compar'd with mee, who am their Epitaph.

Study me then, you who shall lovers bee
At the next world, that is, at the next Spring:
For I am every dead thing,
In whom love wrought new Alchimie.
For his art did expresse
A quintessence even from nothingnesse,
From dull privations, and leane emptinesse:
He ruin'd mee, and I am re-begot
Of absence, darknesse, death; things which are not.

All others, from all things, draw all that's good,
Life, soule, forme, spirit, whence they beeing have;
I, by loves limbecke, am the grave
Of all, that's nothing. Oft a flood
Have wee two wept, and so
Drownd the whole world, us two; oft did we grow
To be two Chaosses, when we did show
Care to ought else; and often absences
Withdrew our soules, and made us carcasses.

But I am by her death, (which word wrongs her)
Of the first nothing, the Elixer grown;
  Were I a man, that I were one,
  I needs must know; I should preferre,
    If I were any beast,
Some ends, some means; Yea plants, yea stones detest,
And love; All, all some properties invest;
If I an ordinary nothing were,
As shadow, a light, and body must be here.

But I am None; nor will my Sunne renew.
You lovers, for whose sake, the lesser Sunne
  At this time to the Goat is runne
  To fetch new lust, and give it you,
    Enjoy your summer all;
Since shee enjoyes her long nights festivall,
Let mee prepare towards her, and let mee call
This houre her Vigill, and her Eve, since this
Both the yeares, and the dayes deep midnight is.

John Donne.

A Valediction: forbidding mourning.

AS virtuous men passe mildly away,
  And whisper to their soules, to goe,
Whilst some of their sad friends doe say,
  The breath goes now, and some say, no:

So let us melt, and make no noise,
  No teare-floods, nor sigh-tempests move,
T'were prophanation of our joyes
  To tell the layetie our love.

Moving of th'earth brings harmes and feares,
  Men reckon what it did and meant,
But trepidation of the spheares,
  Though greater farre, is innocent.

Dull sublunary lovers love
  (Whose soule is sense) cannot admit
Absence, because it doth remove
  Those things which elemented it.

But we by a love, so much refin'd,
  That our selves know not what it is,
Inter-assured of the mind,
  Care lesse, eyes, lips, and hands to misse.

Our two soules therefore, which are one,
  Though I must goe, endure not yet
A breach, but an expansion,
  Like gold to ayery thinnesse beate.

If they be two, they are two so
  As stiffe twin compasses are two,
Thy soule the fixt foot, makes no show
  To move, but doth, if the'other doe.

And though it in the center sit,
  Yet when the other far doth rome,
It leanes, and hearkens after it,
  And growes erect, as that comes home.

Such wilt thou be to mee, who must
  Like th'other foot, obliquely runne;
Thy firmnes makes my circle just,
  And makes me end, where I begunne.

John Donne.

The Extasie.

WHere, like a pillow on a bed,
  A Pregnant banke swel'd up, to rest
The violets reclining head,
  Sat we two, one anothers best.
Our hands were firmely cimented
  With a fast balme, which thence did spring,
Our eye-beames twisted, and did thred
  Our eyes, upon one double string;
So to'entergraft our hands, as yet
  Was all the meanes to make us one,
And pictures in our eyes to get
  Was all our propagation.
As 'twixt two equall Armies, Fate
  Suspends uncertaine victorie,
Our soules, (which to advance their state,
  Were gone out,) hung 'twixt her, and mee.
And whil'st our soules negotiate there,
  Wee like sepulchrall statues lay;
All day, the same our postures were,
  And wee said nothing, all the day.
If any, so by love refin'd,
  That he soules language understood,
And by good love were growen all minde,
  Within convenient distance stood,
He (though he knew not which soule spake,
  Because both meant, both spake the same)
Might thence a new concoction take,
  And part farre purer then he came.
This Extasie doth unperplex
  (We said) and tell us what we love,

Wee see by this, it was not sexe,
  Wee see, we saw not what did move:
But as all severall soules containe
  Mixture of things, they know not what,
Love, these mixt soules, doth mixe againe,
  And makes both one, each this and that.
A single violet transplant,
  The strength, the colour, and the size,
(All which before was poore, and scant,)
  Redoubles still, and multiplies.
When love, with one another so
  Interinanimates two soules,
That abler soule, which thence doth flow,
  Defects of lonelinesse controules.
Wee then, who are this new soule, know,
  Of what we are compos'd, and made,
For, th'Atomies of which we grow,
  Are soules, whom no change can invade.
But O alas, so long, so farre
  Our bodies why doe wee forbeare?
They are ours, though they are not wee, Wee are
  The intelligences, they the spheare.
We owe them thankes, because they thus,
  Did us, to us, at first convay,
Yeelded their forces, sense, to us,
  Nor are drosse to us, but allay.
On man heavens influence workes not so,
  But that it first imprints the ayre,
Soe soule into the soule may flow,
  Though it to body first repaire.
As our blood labours to beget
  Spirits, as like soules as it can,
Because such fingers need to knit

That subtile knot, which makes us man:
So must pure lovers soules descend
T'affections, and to faculties,
Which sense may reach and apprehend,
Else a great Prince in prison lies.
To'our bodies turne wee then, that so
Weake men on love reveal'd may looke;
Loves mysteries in soules doe grow,
But yet the body is his booke.
And if some lover, such as wee,
Have heard this dialogue of one,
Let him still marke us, he shall see
Small change, when we'are to bodies gone.

John Donne.

The Funerall.

WHo ever comes to shroud me, do not harme
Nor question much
That subtile wreath of haire, which crowns my arme;
The mystery, the signe you must not touch,
For'tis my outward Soule,
Viceroy to that, which then to heaven being gone,
Will leave this to controule,
And keepe these limbes, her Provinces, from dissolution.

For if the sinewie thread my braine lets fall
Through every part,
Can tye those parts, and make mee one of all;
These haires which upward grew, and strength and art

Have from a better braine,
Can better do'it; Except she meant that I
By this should know my pain,
As prisoners then are manacled, when thev'are condemn'd to die.

What ere shee meant by'it, bury it with me,
For since I am
Loves martyr, it might breed idolatrie,
If into others hands these Reliques came;
As'twas humility
To afford to it all that a Soule can doe,
So,'tis some bravery,
That since you would save none of mee, I bury some of you.

John Donne.

The Blossome.

Little think'st thou, poore flower,
Whom I have watch'd sixe or seaven dayes,
And seene thy birth, and seene what every houre
Gave to thy growth, thee to this height to raise,
And now dost laugh and triumph on this bough,
Little think'st thou
That it will freeze anon, and that I shall
To morrow finde thee falne, or not at all.

Little think'st thou poore heart
That labour'st yet to nestle thee,
And think'st by hovering here to get a part
In a forbidden or forbidding tree,

And hop'st her stiffenesse by long siege to bow:
Little think'st thou,
That thou to morrow, ere that Sunne doth wake,
Must with this Sunne, and mee a journey take.

But thou which lov'st to bee
Subtile to plague thy selfe, wilt say,
Alas, if you must goe, what's that to mee?
Here lyes my businesse, and here I will stay:
You goe to friends, whose love and meanes present
Various content
To your eyes, eares, and tongue, and every part.
If then your body goe, what need you a heart?

Well then, stay here; but know,
When thou hast stayd and done thy most;
A naked thinking heart, that makes no show,
Is to a woman, but a kinde of Ghost;
How shall shee know my heart; or having none,
Know thee for one?
Practise may make her know some other part,
But take my word, shee doth not know a Heart.

Meet mee at London, then,
Twenty dayes hence, and thou shalt see
Mee fresher, and more fat, by being with men,
Then if I had staid still with her and thee.
For Gods sake, if you can, be you so too:
I would give you
There, to another friend, whom wee shall finde
As glad to have my body, as my minde.

John Donne.

The Relique.

WHen my grave is broke up againe
Some second ghest to entertaine,
(For graves have learn'd that woman-head
To be to more then one a Bed)
And he that digs it, spies
A bracelet of bright haire about the bone,
Will he not let'us alone,
And thinke that there a loving couple lies,
Who thought that this device might be some way
To make their soules, at the last busie day,
Meet at this grave, and make a little stay?

If this fall in a time, or land,
Where mis-devotion doth command,
Then, he that digges us up, will bring
Us, to the Bishop, and the King,
To make us Reliques; then
Thou shalt be a Mary Magdalen, and I
A something else thereby;
All women shall adore us, and some men;
And since at such time, miracles are sought,
I would have that age by this paper taught
What miracles wee harmelesse lovers wrought.

First, we lov'd well and faithfully,
Yet knew not what wee lov'd, nor why,
Difference of sex no more wee knew,
Then our Guardian Angells doe;
Comming and going, wee
Perchance might kisse, but not between those meales;
Our hands ne'r toucht the seales,

Which nature, injur'd by late law, sets free:
These miracles wee did; but now alas,
All measure, and all language, I should passe,
Should I tell what a miracle shee was.

John Donne.

The Prohibition.

TAke heed of loving mee,
At least remember, I forbade it thee;
Not that I shall repaire my unthrifty wast
Of Breath and Blood, upon thy sighes, and teares,
By being to thee then what to me thou wast;
But, so great Joy, our life at once outweares,
Then, least thy love, by my death, frustrate bee,
If thou love mee, take heed of loving mee.

Take heed of hating mee,
Or too much triumph in the Victorie.
Not that I shall be mine owne officer,
And hate with hate againe retaliate;
But thou wilt lose the stile of conquerour,
If I, thy conquest, perish by thy hate.
Then, least my being nothing lessen thee,
If thou hate mee, take heed of hating mee.

Yet, love and hate mee too,
So, these extreames shall neithers office doe;
Love mee, that I may die the gentler way;
Hate mee, because thy love is too great for mee;
Or let these two, themselves, not me decay;
So shall I, live, thy Stage, not triumph bee;
Lest thou thy love and hate and mee undoe,
To let mee live, O love and hate mee too.

John Donne.

The Expiration.

SO, so, breake off this last lamenting kisse,
Which sucks two soules, and vapors Both away,
Turne thou ghost that way, and let mee turne this,
And let our selves benight our happiest day,
We ask'd none leave to love; nor will we owe
Any, so cheape a death, as saying, Goe;

Goe; and if that word have not quite kil'd thee,
Ease mee with death, by bidding mee goe too.
Or, if it have, let my word worke on mee,
And a just office on a murderer doe.
Except it be too late, to kill me so,
Being double dead, going, and bidding, goe.

John Donne.

Absence.

ABsence heare my protestation
Against thy strengthe
Distance and lengthe,
Doe what thou canst for alteration:
For harts of truest mettall
Absence doth joyne, and time doth settle.

Who loves a Mistris of right quality,
His mind hath founde
Affections grounde
Beyond time, place, and all mortality:
To harts that cannot vary
Absence is present, time doth tary:

My Sences want their outward motion
Which now within
Reason doth win,
Redoubled by her secret notion:
Like rich men that take pleasure
In hidinge more then handling treasure.

By absence this good means I gaine
That I can catch her
Where none can watch her
In some close corner of my braine:
There I embrace and kiss her,
And so enjoye her, and so misse her.

John Hoskins.

On his Mistris, the Queen *of* Bohemia.

YOu meaner *Beauties* of the *Night*,
That poorly satisfie our *Eies*
More by your *number*, then your *light*,
You *Common-people* of the *Skies*;
What are you when the *Sun* shall rise?

You Curious Chanters of the Wood,
That warble forth *Dame Natures* layes,
Thinking your *Voyces* understood
By your weake *accents*; what's your praise
When *Philomell* her voyce shal raise?

You *Violets*, that first apeare,
By your *pure purpel mantels* knowne,
Like the proud *Virgins* of the *yeare*,
As if the *Spring* were all your own;
What are you when the *Rose is blowne*?

So, when *my Mistris* shal be *seene*
In *Form* and *Beauty* of her *mind*,
By *Vertue* first, then *Choyce* a *Queen*,
Tell me, if *she* were not design'd
  Th' *Eclypse* and *Glory* of her kind?

Sir Henry Wotton.

Loves Victory.

VIctorious beauty, though your eyes
  Are able to subdue an hoast,
  And therefore are unlike to boast
The taking of a little prize,
Do not a single heart dispise.

It came alone, but yet so arm'd
  With former love, I durst have sworne
  That where a privy coat was worne,
With characters of beauty charm'd,
Thereby it might have scapt unharm'd.

But neither steele nor stony breast
  Are proofe against those lookes of thine,
  Nor can a Beauty lesse divine
Of any heart be long possest,
Where thou pretend st an interest.

Thy Conquest in regard of me
  Alasse is small, but in respect
  Of her that did my Love protect,
Were it divulged, deserv'd to be
Recorded for a Victory.

And such a one, as some that view
  Her lovely face perhaps may say,
  Though you have stolen my heart away,
If all your servants prove not true,
May steale a heart or two from you.

Aurelian Townshend.

Upon kinde and true Love.

'TIs not how witty, nor how free,
  Nor yet how beautifull she be,
But how much kinde and true to me.
Freedome and Wit none can confine,
And Beauty like the Sun doth shine,
But kinde and true are onely mine.

Let others with attention sit,
To listen, and admire her wit,
That is a rock where Ile not split
Let others dote upon her eyes,
And burn their hearts for sacrifice,
Beauty's a calm where danger lyes.

But Kinde and True have been long tried
A harbour where we may confide,
And safely there at anchor ride.
From change of winds there we are free,
And need not feare Storme's tyrannie,
Nor Pirat, though a Prince he be.

Aurelian Townshend.

Elegy over a Tomb.

MUst I then see, alas! eternal night
Sitting upon those fairest eyes,
And closing all those beams, which once did rise
So radiant and bright,
That light and heat in them to us did prove
Knowledge and Love?

Oh, if you did delight no more to stay
Upon this low and earthly stage,
But rather chose an endless heritage,
Tell us at least, we pray,
Where all the beauties that those ashes ow'd
Are now bestow'd?

Doth the Sun now his light with yours renew?
Have Waves the curling of your hair?
Did you restore unto the Sky and Air,
The red, and white, and blew?
Have you vouchsafed to flowers since your death
That sweetest breath?

Had not Heav'ns Lights else in their houses slept,
Or to some private life retir'd?
Must not the Sky and Air have else conspir'd,
And in their Regions wept?
Must not each flower else the earth could breed
Have been a weed?

But thus enrich'd may we not yield some cause
Why they themselves lament no more?
That must have changed the course they held before,
And broke their proper Laws,
Had not your beauties giv'n this second birth
To Heaven and Earth?

Tell us, for Oracles must still ascend,
For those that crave them at your tomb:
Tell us, where are those beauties now become,
And what they now intend:
Tell us, alas, that cannot tell our grief,
Or hope relief.

Lord Herbert of Cherbury.

An Ode upon a Question moved, whether Love should continue for ever?

HAving interr'd her Infant-birth,
The watry ground that late did mourn,
Was strew'd with flow'rs for the return
Of the wish'd Bridegroom of the earth.

The well accorded Birds did sing
Their hymns unto the pleasant time,
And in a sweet consorted chime
Did welcom in the chearful Spring.

To which, soft whistles of the Wind,
And warbling murmurs of a Brook,
And vari'd notes of leaves that shook,
An harmony of parts did bind.

While doubling joy unto each other,
All in so rare concent was shown,
No happiness that came alone,
Nor pleasure that was not another.

When with a love none can express,
  That mutually happy pair,
  Melander and *Celinda* fair,
The season with their loves did bless.

Walking thus towards a pleasant Grove,
  What did, it seem'd, in new delight
  The pleasures of the time unite,
To give a triumph to their love,

They stay'd at last, and on the Grass
  Reposed so, as o'r his breast
  She bow'd her gracious head to rest,
Such a weight as no burden was.

While over eithers compassed waste
  Their folded arms were so compos'd,
  As if in straitest bonds inclos'd,
They suffer'd for joys they did taste.

Long their fixt eyes to Heaven bent,
  Unchanged, they did never move,
  As if so great and pure a love
No Glass but it could represent.

When with a sweet, though troubled look,
  She first brake silence, saying, Dear friend,
  O that our love might take no end,
Or never had beginning took!

I speak not this with a false heart,
  (Wherewith his hand she gently strain'd)
  Or that would change a love maintain'd
With so much faith on either part.

Nay, I protest, though Death with his
  Worst Counsel should divide us here,
  His terrors could not make me fear,
To come where your lov'd presence is.

Only if loves fire with the breath
  Of life be kindled, I doubt,
  With our last air 'twill be breath'd out,
And quenched with the cold of death.

That if affection be a line,
  Which is clos'd up in our last hour;
  Oh how 'twould grieve me, any pow'r
Could force so dear a love as mine

She scarce had done, when his shut eyes
  An inward joy did represent,
  To hear *Celinda* thus intent
To a love he so much did prize.

Then with a look, it seem'd, deny'd
  All earthly pow'r but hers, yet so,
  As if to her breath he did ow
This borrow'd life, he thus repli'd;

O you, wherein, they say, Souls rest,
  Till they descend pure heavenly fires,
  Shall lustful and corrupt desires
With your immortal seed be blest?

And shall our Love, so far beyond
  That low and dying appetite,
  And which so chast desires unite,
Not hold in an eternal bond?

Is it, because we should decline,
  And wholly from our thoughts exclude
  Objects that may the sense delude,
And study only the Divine?

No sure, for if none can ascend
  Ev'n to the visible degree
  Of things created, how should we
The invisible comprehend?

Or rather since that Pow'r exprest
  His greatness in his works alone,
  B'ing here best in his Creatures known,
Why is he not lov'd in them best?

But is't not true, which you pretend,
  That since our love and knowledge here,
  Only as parts of life appear,
So they with it should take their end.

O no, Belov'd, I am most sure,
  Those vertuous habits we acquire,
  As being with the Soul intire,
Must with it evermore endure.

For if where sins and vice reside,
  We find so foul a guilt remain,
  As never dying in his stain,
Still punish'd in the Soul doth bide.

Much more that true and real joy,
  Which in a vertuous love is found,
  Must be more solid in its ground,
Then Fate or Death can e'r destroy.

Else should our Souls in vain elect,
And vainer yet were Heavens laws,
When to an everlasting Cause
They gave a perishing Effect.

Nor here on earth then, nor above,
Our good affection can impair,
For where God doth admit the fair,
Think you that he excludeth Love?

These eyes again then, eyes shall see,
And hands again these hands enfold,
And all chast pleasures can be told
Shall with us everlasting be.

For if no use of sense remain
When bodies once this life forsake,
Or they could no delight partake,
Why should they ever rise again?

And if every imperfect mind
Make love the end of knowledge here,
How perfect will our love be, where
All imperfection is refin'd?

Let then no doubt, *Celinda*, touch,
Much less your fairest mind invade,
Were not our souls immortal made,
Our equal loves can make them such.

So when one wing can make no way,
Two joyned can themselves dilate,
So can two persons propagate,
When singly either would decay.

So when from hence we shall be gone,
And be no more, nor you, nor I,
As one anothers mystery,
Each shall be both, yet both but one.

This said, in her up-lifted face,
Her eyes which did that beauty crown,
Were like two starrs, that having faln down,
Look up again to find their place:

While such a moveless silent peace
Did seize on their becalmed sense,
One would have thought some influence
Their ravish'd spirits did possess.

Lord Herbert of Cherbury.

Mediocrity in love rejected.

GIve me more Love, or more Disdain;
The Torrid, or the Frozen Zone
Bring equall ease unto my paine;
The Temperate affords me none:
Either extreme, of Love, or Hate,
Is sweeter than a calme estate.

Give me a storme; if it be Love,
Like *Danae* in that golden showre
I swim in pleasure; if it prove
Disdain, that Torrent will devour
My Vulture-hopes; and he's possest
Of Heaven, that's but from Hell releast:
Then crown my joyes, or cure my pain;
Give me more Love, or more Disdain.

Thomas Carew.

To my inconstant Mistris.

WHen thou, poore excommunicate
From all the joyes of love, shalt see
The full reward, and glorious fate,
Which my strong faith shall purchase me,
Then curse thine owne inconstancy.

A fayrer hand than thine, shall cure
That heart, which thy false oathes did wound;
And to my soul, a soul more pure
Than thine, shall by Loves hand be bound,
And both with equall glory crown'd.

Then shalt thou weepe, entreat, complain
To Love, as I did once to thee;
When all thy teares shall be as vain
As mine were then, for thou shalt bee
Damn'd for thy false Apostasie.

Thomas Carew.

A deposition from love.

I Was foretold, your rebell sex,
Nor love, nor pitty knew;
And with what scorn you use to vex
Poor hearts that humbly sue;
Yet I believ'd, to crown our pain,
Could we the fortress win,
The happy Lovei sure should gain
A Paradise within:
I thought Loves plagues, like Dragons sate,
Only to fright us at the gate.

But I did enter, and enjoy
 What happy Lovers prove;
For I could kiss, and sport, and toy,
 And taste those sweets of love;
Which had they but a lasting state,
 Or if in *Celia's* brest
The force of love might not abate,
 Jove were too mean a guest.
But now her breach of faith, farre more
Afflicts, than did her scorn before.

Hard fate! to have been once possest,
 As victor, of a heart
Atchiev'd with labour, and unrest,
 And then forc'd to depart.
If the stout Foe will not resigne
 When I besiege a Town,
I lose, but what was never mine;
 But he that is cast down
From enjoy'd beauty, feels a woe,
Only deposed Kings can know.

Thomas Carew.

Ingratefull beauty threatned.

KNow *Celia*, (since thou art so proud,)
 'Twas I that gave thee thy renown:
Thou hadst, in the forgotten crowd
 Of common beauties, liv'd unknown,
Had not my verse exhal'd thy name,
And with it ympt the wings of fame.

That killing power is none of thine,
I gave it to thy voyce, and eyes:
Thy sweets, thy graces, all are mine;
Thou art my star, shin'st in my skies;
Then dart not from thy borrowed sphere
Lightning on him that fixt thee there.

Tempt me with such affrights no more,
Lest what I made, I uncreate:
Let fools thy mystique forms adore,
Ile know thee in thy mortall state;
Wise Poets that wrap'd Truth in tales,
Knew her themselves through all her vailes.

Thomas Carew.

Eternity of Love protested.

HOw ill doth he deserve a Lovers name,
Whose pale weak flame
Cannot retain
His heat in spight of absence or disdain;
But doth at once, like paper set on fire,
Burn and expire;
True love can never change his seat,
Nor did he ever love, that could retreat

That noble flame, which my brest keeps alive,
Shall still survive,
When my soule's fled;
Nor shall my love dye, when my bodye's dead,
That shall wait on me to the lower shade.
And never fade:
My very ashes in their urn,
Shall, like a hallowed Lamp, for ever burn.

Thomas Carew.

To a Lady that desired I would love her.

NOw you have freely given me leave to love,
What will you doe?
Shall I your mirth, or passion move,
When I begin to wooe;
Will you torment, or scorn, or love me too?

Each petty beauty can disdain, and I,
Spight of your hate,
Without your leave can see, and dye,
Dispence a nobler Fate,
Tis easie to destroy, you may create.

Then give me leave to love, and love me too,
Not with designe
To rayse, as Loves curst Rebels doe,
When puling Poets whine,
Fame to their beauty, from their blubbr'd eyn.

Grief is a puddle, and reflects not clear
Your beauties rayes;
Joyes are pure streames, your eyes appear
Sullen in sadder layes,
In cheerfull numbers they shine bright with prayse.

Which shall not mention, to express you fayr,
Wounds, flames, and darts,
Storms in your brow, nets in your hair,
Suborning all your parts,
Or to betray, or torture captive hearts.

I'le make your eyes like morning Suns appear,
As mild, and fair;
Your brow as Crystal smooth, and clear,
And your dishevell'd hayr
Shall flow like a calm Region of the Ayr.

Rich Nature's store, (which is the Poet's Treasure)
I'le spend, to dress
Your beauties, if your mine of Pleasure
In equall thankfulness
You but unlock, so we each other bless.

Thomas Carew.

A Song.

ASk me no more where *Jove* bestowes,
When *June* is past, the fading rose:
For in your beauties orient deep,
These Flowers as in their causes sleep.

Ask me no more whither doe stray
The golden Atomes of the day:
For in pure love heaven did prepare
Those powders to inrich your hair.

Ask me no more whither doth hast
The Nightingale, when *May* is past:
For in your sweet dividing throat
She winters, and keeps warm her note.

Ask me no more where those starres light,
That downwards fall in dead of night:
For in your eyes they sit, and there,
Fixed, become as in their sphere.

Ask me no more if East or West,
The Phenix builds her spicy nest:
For unto you at last she flyes,
And in your fragrant bosome dies.

Thomas Carew.

To Roses in the bosome of Castara.

YEe blushing Virgins happy are
In the chaste Nunn'ry of her brests,
For hee'd prophane so chaste a faire,
Who ere should call them *Cupids* nests.

Transplanted thus how bright yee grow;
How rich a perfume doe yee yeeld?
In some close garden, Cowslips so
Are sweeter then i' th' open field.

In those white cloysters live secure
From the rude blasts of wanton breath,
Each houre more innocent and pure,
Till you shall wither into death.

Then that which living gave you roome,
Your glorious sepulcher shall be,
There wants no marble for a tombe,
Whose brest hath marble beene to me.

William Habington.

Sonnet.

OF thee (kind boy) I ask no red and white
to make up my delight,
no odd becomming graces,
Black eyes, or little know-not-whats, in faces;
Make me but mad enough, give me good store
Of Love, for her I court,
I ask no more,
'Tis love in love that makes the sport.

There's no such thing as that we beauty call,
it is meer cousenage all;
for though some long ago
Like 't certain colours mingled so and so,
That doth not tie me now from chusing new,
If I a fancy take
To black and blue,
That fancy doth it beauty make.

Tis not the meat, but 'tis the appetite
makes eating a delight,
and if I like one dish
More then another, that a Pheasant is;
What in our watches, that in us is found,
So to the height and nick
We up be wound,
No matter by what hand or trick.

Sir John Suckling.

Sonnet.

OH ! for some honest Lovers ghost,
Some kind unbodied post
Sent from the shades below.
I strangely long to know
Whether the nobler Chaplets wear,
Those that their mistresse scorn did bear,
Or those that were us'd kindly.

For what-so-e're they tell us here
To make those sufferings dear,
'Twill there I fear be found,
That to the being crown'd,
T' have lov'd alone will not suffice,
Unlesse we alsc have been wise,
And have our Loves enjoy'd.

What posture can we think him in,
That here unlov'd agen
Departs, and 's thither gone
Where each sits by his own ?
Or how can that *Elizium* be
Where I my Mistresse still must see
Circled in others Armes ?

For there the Judges all are just,
And *Sophonisba* must
Be his whom she held dear ;
Not his who lov'd her here
The sweet *Philoclea* since she dy'de
Lies by her *Pirocles* his side,
Not by *Amphialus*.

Some Bayes (perchance) or Myrtle bough,
For difference crowns the brow
Of those kind souls that were
The noble Martyrs here;
And if that be the onely odds
(As who can tell) ye kinder Gods,
Give me the Woman here.

Sir John Suckling.

MY dearest Rival, least our Love
Should with excentrique motion move,
Before it learn to go astray,
Wee'l teach and set it in a way,
And such directions give unto't,
That it shall never wander foot.
Know first then, we will serve as true
For one poor smile, as we would do
If we had what our higher flame,
Or our vainer wish could frame.
Impossible shall be our hope;
And Love shall onely have his scope
To joyn with Fancy now and then,
And think what reason would condemn:
And on these grounds wee'l love as true,
As if they were most sure t'ensue:
And chastly for these things wee'l stay,
As if to morrow were the day.
Mean time we two will teach our hearts
In Loves burdens bear their parts:
Thou first shall sigh, and say shee's fair;
And I'le still answer, past compare.

Thou shalt set out each part o' th face,
While I extol each little grace;
Thou shalt be ravisht at her wit;
And I, that she so governs it:
Thou shalt like well that hand, that eye,
That lip, that look, that majesty;
And in good language them adore:
While I want words, and do it more.
Yea we will sit and sigh a while,
And with soft thoughts some time beguile;
But straight again break out and praise
All we had done before new-waies.
Thus will we do till paler death
Come with a warrant for our breath,
And then whose fate shall be to die
First of us two, by Legacy
Shall all his store bequeath, and give
His love to him that shall survive;
For no one stock can ever serve
To love so much as shee'l deserve.

Sir John Suckling.

Song.

OUt upon it, I have lov'd
Three whole days together;
And am like to love three more,
If it prove fair weather.

Time shall moult away his wings
Ere he shall discover
In the whole wide world agen
Such a constant Lover.

But the spite on't is, no praise
  Is due at all to me:
Love with me had made no staies
  Had it any been but she.

Had it any been but she
  And that very Face,
There had been at least ere this
  A dozen dozen in her place.

Sir John Suckling.

To Cynthia.

On concealment of her beauty.

DO not conceale thy radiant eyes,
The starre-light of serenest skies,
Least wanting of their heavenly light,
They turne to *Chaos* endlesse night.

Do not conceale those tresses faire,
The silken snares of thy curl'd haire,
Least finding neither gold, nor Ore,
The curious Silke-worme worke no more.

Do not conceale those brests of thine,
More snowe white then the Apenine,
Least if there be like cold or frost,
The Lilly be for ever lost.

Do not conceale that fragrant scent,
Thy breath, which to all flowers hath lent
Perfumes, least it being supprest,
No spices growe in all the East.

Do not conceale thy heavenly voice,
Which makes the hearts of gods rejoyce,
Least Musicke hearing no such thing,
The Nightingale forget to sing.

Do not conceale, not yet eclipse
Thy pearly teeth with Corrall lips,
Least that the Seas cease to bring forth
Gems, which from thee have all their worth.

Do not conceale no beauty grace,
That's either in thy minde or face,
Least vertue overcome by vice,
Make men beleeve no Paradice.

Sir Francis Kynaston.

Song.

NOe more unto my thoughts appeare,
Att least appeare lesse fayre,
For crazy tempers justly feare
The goodnesse of the ayre;

Whilst your pure Image hath a place
In my impurer Mynde,
Your very shaddow is the glasse
Where my defects I finde.

Shall I not fly that brighter light
Which makes my fyres looke pale,
And put that vertue out of sight
Which makes myne none att all?

No, no, your picture doeth impart
  Such valew I not wish
The native worth to any heart
  That 's unadorn'd with this.

Though poorer in desert I make
  My selfe whilst I admyre,
The fuell which from hope I take
  I give to my desire.

If this flame lighted from your Eyes
  The subject doe calcine,
A Heart may bee your sacrifice
  Too weake to bee your shrine.

Sidney Godolphin.

Song.

To the tune of, In fayth I cannot keepe my fathers sheepe.

CLoris, it is not thy disdaine
  Can ever cover with dispaire
  Or in cold ashes hide that care
Which I have fedd with soe long paine,
I may perhaps myne eyes refraine
And fruiteless wordes noe more impart,
But yet still serve, still serve thee in my hearte.

What though I spend my haplesse dayes
  In finding entertainements out,
  Carelesse of what I goe about,
Or seeke my peace in skillfull wayes
Applying to my Eyes new rays
Of Beauty, and another flame
Unto my Heart, my heart is still the same.

Tis true that I could love noe face
  Inhabited by cold disdayne,
  Taking delight in others paine.
Thy lookes are full of native grace;
Since then by chance scorne there hath place,
Tis to be hop't I may remove
This scorne one day, one day by Endless Love.

Sidney Godolphin.

Upon Phillis *walking in a morning before Sun-rising.*

THe sluggish morne as yet undrest,
  My *Phillis* brake from out her East;
As if shee'd made a match to run
With *Venus*, Usher to the sun.
The Trees like yeomen of her guard,
Serving more for pomp then ward,
Rankt on each side with loyall duty,
Weave branches to enclose her beauty.
The Plants whose luxury was lopt,
Or age with crutches underpropt;
Whose wooden carkases are growne
To be but coffins of their owne;
Revive, and at her generall dole
Each receives his ancient soule:
The winged Choristers began
To chirp their Mattins: and the Fan
Of whistling winds like Organs plai'd,

Untill their Voluntaries made
The wakened earth in Odours rise
To be her morning Sacrifice.
The flowers, call'd out of their beds,
Start, and raise up their drowsie heads;
And he that for their colour seekes,
May find it vaulting in her cheekes,
Where Roses mixe: no Civil War
Betweene her *Yorke* and *Lancaster*.
The Marigold whose Courtiers face
Ecchoes the Sun, and doth unlace
Her at his rise, at his full stop
Packs and shuts up her gaudy shop,
Mistakes her cue, and doth display:
Thus *Philis* antedates the day.
  These miracles had cramp't the Sunne,
Who thinking that his kingdom 's wonne,
Powders with light his freezled lockes,
To see what Saint his lustre mocks.
The trembling leaves through which he plai'd,
Dapling the walke with light and shade,
Like Lattice-windowes, give the spie
Roome but to peep with halfe an eye;
Lest her full Orb his sight should dim,
And bid us all good-night in him,
Till she would spend a gentle ray
To force us a new fashion'd day.
But what religious Paulsie 's this
Which makes the boughs divest their bliss?
And that they might her foot-steps strawe,
Drop their leaves with shivering awe?
Phillis perceives, and (least her stay
Should wed October unto May;

And as her beauty caus'd a Spring,
Devotion might an Autumne bring)
With-drew her beames, yet made no night,
But left the Sun her Curate-light.

John Cleveland.

Song.

THe Lark now leaves his watry Nest
And climbing, shakes his dewy Wings;
He takes this Window for the East;
And to implore your Light, he Sings,
Awake, awake, the Morn will never rise,
Till she can dress her Beauty at your Eies.

The Merchant bowes unto the Seamans Star,
The Ploughman from the Sun his Season takes;
But still the Lover wonders what they are,
Who look for day before his Mistress wakes.
Awake, awake, break through your Vailes of Lawne!
Then draw your Curtains, and begin the Dawne.

Sir William Davenant.

Song.

Endimion Porter, *and* Olivia.

Olivia.

BEfore we shall again behold
In his diurnal race the Worlds great Eye,
We may as silent be and cold,
As are the shades where buried Lovers ly.

Endimion.

Olivia 'tis no fault of Love
To loose our selves in death, but O, I fear,
When Life and Knowledge is above
Restor'd to us, I shall not know thee there.

Olivia.

Call it not Heaven (my Love) where we
Our selves shall see, and yet each other miss:
So much of Heaven I find in thee
As, thou unknown, all else privation is.

Endimion.

Why should we doubt, before we go
To find the Knowledge which shall ever last,
That we may there each other know?
Can future Knowledge quite destroy the past?

Olivia.

When at the Bowers in the Elizian shade
I first arrive, I shall examine where
They dwel, who love the highest Vertue made?
For I am sure to find *Endimion* there.

Endimion.

From this vext World when we shall both retire,
Where all are Lovers, and where all rejoyce;
I need not seek thee in the Heavenly Quire;
For I shall know *Olivia* by her Voice.

Sir William Davenant.

Loves Horoscope.

LOve, brave Vertues younger Brother,
Erst hath made my Heart a Mother,
Shee consults the conscious Spheares,
To calculate her young sons yeares.
Shee askes if sad, or saving powers,
Gave Omen to his infant howers,
Shee askes each starre that then stood by,
If poore Love shall live or dy.

Ah my Heart, is that the way?
Are these the Beames that rule thy Day?
Thou know'st a Face in whose each looke,
Beauty layes ope Loves Fortune-booke;
On whose faire revolutions wait
The obsequious motions of Loves fate;
Ah my Heart, her eyes and shee,
Have taught thee new Astrologie.
How e're Loves native houres were set,
What ever starry Synod met,
'Tis in the mercy of her eye,
If poore Love shall live or dye.

If those sharpe Rayes putting on
Points of Death bid Love be gon,
(Though the Heavens in counsell sate,
To crowne an uncontrouled Fate,
Though their best Aspects twin'd upon
The kindest Constellation,
Cast amorous glances on his Birth,
And whisper'd the confederate Earth

To pave his pathes with all the good
That warms the Bed of youth and blood ;)
Love ha's no plea against her eye,
Beauty frownes, and Love must dye.

But if her milder influence move,
And gild the hopes of humble Love :
(Though heavens inauspicious eye
Lay blacke on Loves Nativitie ;
Though every Diamond in *Joves* crowne
Fixt his forehead to a frowne,)
Her Eye a strong appeale can give,
Beauty smiles and Love shall live.

O if Love shall live, ô where,
But in her Eye, or in her Eare,
In her Brest, or in her Breath,
Shall I hide poore Love from Death ?
For in the life ought else can give,
Love shall dye, although he live.

Or if Love shall dye, ô where,
But in her Eye, or in her Eare,
In her Breath, or in her Breast,
Shall I Build his funerall Nest ?
While Love shall thus entombed lye,
Love shall live, although he dye.

Richard Crashaw.

Wishes.

To his (supposed) Mistresse.

WHo ere she be,
That not impossible she
That shall command my heart and me;

Where ere she lye,
Lock't up from mortall Eye,
In shady leaves of Destiny;

Till that ripe Birth
Of studied fate stand forth,
And teach her faire steps to our Earth;

Till that Divine
Idæa, take a shrine
Of Chrystall flesh, through which to shine;

Meet you her my wishes,
Bespeake her to my blisses,
And be ye call'd my absent kisses.

I wish her Beauty,
That owes not all his Duty
To gaudy Tire, or glistring shoo-ty.

Something more than
Taffata or Tissew can,
Or rampant feather, or rich fan.

More than the spoyle
Of shop, or silkewormes Toyle,
Or a bought blush, or a set smile.

A face thats best
By its owne beauty drest,
And can alone command the rest.

A face made up,
Out of no other shop
Than what natures white hand sets ope.

A cheeke where Youth,
And Blood, with Pen of Truth
Write, what the Reader sweetly ru'th.

A Cheeke where growes
More than a Morning Rose:
Which to no Boxe his being owes.

Lipps, where all Day
A lovers kisse may play,
Yet carry nothing thence away.

Lookes that oppresse
Their richest Tires, but dresse
And cloath their simplest Nakednesse.

Eyes, that displaces
The Neighbour Diamond, and out-faces
That Sunshine, by their own sweet Graces.

Tresses, that weare
Jewells, but to declare
How much themselves more pretious are.

Whose native Ray,
Can tame the wanton Day
Of Gems, that in their bright shades play.

Each Ruby there,
Or Pearle that dare appeare,
Be its own blush, be its own Teare.

A well tam'd Heart,
For whose more noble smart,
Love may be long chusing a Dart.

Eyes, that bestow
Full quivers on loves Bow;
Yet pay lesse Arrowes than they owe.

Smiles, that can warme
The blood, yet teach a charme,
That Chastity shall take no harme.

Blushes, that bin
The burnish of no sin,
Nor flames of ought too hot within.

Joyes, that confesse,
Vertue their Mistresse,
And have no other head to dresse.

Feares, fond and slight,
As the coy Brides, when Night
First does the longing Lover right.

Teares, quickly fled,
And vaine, as those are shed
For a dying Maydenhead.

Dayes, that need borrow,
No part of their good Morrow,
From a fore spent night of sorrow.

Dayes, that in spight
Of Darkenesse, by the Light
Of a cleere mind are Day all Night.

Nights, sweet as they,
Made short by Lovers play,
Yet long by th' absence of the Day.

Life, that dares send
A challenge to his end,
And when it comes say *Welcome Friend.*

Sydnæan showers
Of sweet discourse, whose powers
Can Crown old Winters head with flowers.

Soft silken Hours,
Open sunnes, shady Bowers;
'Bove all, Nothing within that lowers.

What ere Delight
Can make Dayes forehead bright,
Or give Downe to the Wings of Night.

In her whole frame,
Have Nature all the Name,
Art and ornament the shame.

Her flattery,
Picture and Poesy,
Her counsell her owne vertue be.

I wish, her store
Of worth may leave her poore
Of wishes: And I wish —— No more.

Now if Time knowes
That her whose radiant Browes
Weave them a Garland of my vowes,

Her whose just Bayes,
My future hopes can raise,
A trophie to her present praise;

Her that dares be,
What these Lines wish to see.
I seeke no further, it is she.

'Tis she, and here
Lo I uncloath and cleare,
My wishes cloudy Character.

May she enjoy it,
Whose merit dare apply it,
But Modesty dares still deny it.

Such worth as this is
Shall fixe my flying wishes,
And determine them to kisses.

Let her full Glory,
My fancyes, fly before ye,
Be ye my fictions; But her story.

Richard Crashaw.

To Lucasta,

Going beyond the Seas.

IF to be absent were to be
Away from thee;
Or that when I am gone,
You or I were alone;
Then my *Lucasta* might I crave
Pity from blustring winde, or swallowing wave.

But I'le not sigh one blast or gale
To swell my saile,
Or pay a teare to swage
The foaming blew-Gods rage;
For whether he will let me passe
Or no, I'm still as happy as I was.

Though Seas and Land be 'twixt us both,
Our Faith and Troth,
Like separated soules,
All time and space controules:
Above the highest sphere wee meet
Unseene, unknowne, and greet as Angels greet.

So then we doe anticipate
Our after-fate,
And are alive i' th' skies
If thus our lips and eyes
Can speake like spirits unconfin'd
In Heav'n, their earthy bodies left behind.

Richard Lovelace.

To Lucasta,

Going to the Warres.

TEll me not (Sweet) I am unkinde,
That from the Nunnerie
Of thy chaste breast, and quiet minde,
To Warre and Armes I flie.

True; a new Mistresse now I chase,
The first Foe in the Field;
And with a stronger Faith imbrace
A Sword, a Horse, a Shield.

Yet this Inconstancy is such,
As you too shall adore;
I could not love thee (Deare) so much,
Lov'd I not Honour more.

Richard Lovelace.

Gratiana *dauncing and singing.*

SEe! with what constant Motion
Even, and glorious, as the Sunne,
Gratiana steeres that Noble Frame,
Soft as her breast, sweet as her voyce
That gave each winding Law and poyze,
And swifter then the wings of Fame,

She beat the happy Pavement
By such a Starre made Firmament,
Which now no more the Roofe envies;
But swells up high with *Atlas* ev'n,
Bearing the brighter, nobler Heav'n,
And in her, all the Dieties.

Each step trod out a Lovers thought
And the Ambitious hopes he brought,
Chain'd to her brave feet with such arts;
Such sweet command, and gentle awe,
As when she ceas'd, we sighing saw
The floore lay pav'd with broken hearts.

So did she move; so did she sing
Like the Harmonious spheres that bring
Unto their Rounds their musick's ayd;
Which she performed such a way,
As all th' inamour'd world will say
The *Graces* daunced, and *Apollo* play'd.

Richard Lovelace.

The Scrutinie.

WHy should you sweare I am forsworn,
Since thine I vow'd to be?
Lady it is already Morn,
And 'twas last night I swore to thee
That fond impossibility.

Have I not lov'd thee much and long,
A tedious twelve houres space?
I must all other Beauties wrong,
And rob thee of a new imbrace;
Could I still dote upon thy Face.

Not, but all joy in thy browne haire,
By others may be found;
But I must search the black and faire
Like skilfull Minerallist's that sound
For Treasure in un-plow'd-up ground.

Then, if when I have lov'd my round,
Thou prov'st the pleasant she;
With spoyles of meaner Beauties crown'd,
I laden will returne to thee,
Ev'n sated with Varietie.

Richard Lovelace.

To Althea,

From Prison.

WHen Love with unconfined wings
  Hovers within my Gates;
And my divine *Althea* brings
  To whisper at the Grates:
When I lye tangled in her haire,
  And fetterd to her eye;
The *Birds*, that wanton in the Aire,
  Know no such Liberty.

When flowing Cups run swiftly round
  With no allaying *Thames*,
Our carelesse heads with Roses bound,
  Our hearts with Loyall Flames;
When thirsty griefe in Wine we steepe,
  When Healths and draughts go free,
Fishes that tipple in the Deepe,
  Know no such Libertie.

When (like committed Linnets) I
  With shriller throat shall sing
The sweetnes, Mercy, Majesty,
  And glories of my KING;
When I shall voyce aloud, how Good
  He is, how Great should be;
Inlarged Winds that curle the Flood,
  Know no such Liberty.

Stone Walls doe not a Prison make,
Nor I'ron bars a Cage;
Mindes innocent and quiet take
That for an Hermitage;
If I have freedome in my Love,
And in my soule am free;
Angels alone that sore above,
Injoy such Liberty.

Richard Lovelace.

To Amoret *gone from him.*

FAncy, and I, last Evening walkt,
And, *Amoret*, of thee we talkt;
The West just then had stolne the Sun,
And his last blushes were begun:
We sate, and markt how every thing
Did mourne his absence; How the Spring
That smil'd, and curl'd about his beames,
Whilst he was here, now check'd her streames:
The wanton Eddies of her face
Were taught lesse noise, and smoother grace;
And in a slow, sad channell went,
Whisp'ring the banks their discontent:
The carelesse ranks of flowers that spread
Their perfum'd bosomes to his head,
And with an open, free Embrace,
Did entertaine his beamy face;
Like absent friends point to the West,
And on that weake reflection feast.

If Creatures then that have no sence,
But the loose tye of influence,
(Though fate, and time each day remove
Those things that element their love)
At such vast distance can agree,
  Why, *Amoret*, why should not wee.

Henry Vaughan.

The Call.

Romira, stay,
And run not thus like a young Roe away,
No enemie
Pursues thee (foolish girle) tis onely I,
I'le keep off harms,
If thou'l be pleas'd to garrison mine arms;
What dost thou fear
I'le turn a Traitour? may these Roses here
To palenesse shred,
And Lilies stand disguised in new Red,
If that I lay
A snare, wherein thou wouldst not gladly stay;
See see the Sunne
Does slowly to his azure Lodging run,
Come sit but here
And presently hee'l quit our Hemisphere,
So still among
Lovers, time is too short or else too long;
Here will we spin
Legends for them that have Love Martyrs been,
Here on this plain
Wee'l talk *Narcissus* to a flour again;

Come here, and chose
On which of these proud plats thou would repose,
Here maist thou shame
The rusty Violets, with the Crimson flame
Of either cheek,
And Primroses white as thy fingers seek,
Nay, thou maist prove
That mans most Noble Passion is to Love.

John Hall.

An Epicurean Ode.

Since that this thing we call the world
By chance on Atomes is begot,
Which though in dayly motions hurld,
Yet weary not,
How doth it prove
Thou art so fair and I in Love?

Since that the soul doth onely lie
Immers'd in matter, chaind in sense,
How can *Romira* thou and I
With both dispence?
And thus ascend
In higher flights then wings can lend.

Since man's but pasted up of Earth,
And ne're was cradled in the skies,
What *Terra Lemnia* gave thee birth?
What Diamond eyes?
Or thou alone
To tell what others were, came down?

John Hall.

The Repulse.

NOt that by this disdain
I am releas'd,
And freed from thy tyrannick chain,
Do I my self think blest;

Nor that thy Flame shall burn
No more; for know
That I shall into ashes turn,
Before this fire doth so.

Nor yet that unconfin'd
I now may rove,
And with new beauties please my mind;
But that thou ne'r didst love:

For since thou hast no part
Felt of this flame,
Lonely from thy tyrant heart
Repuls'd, not banish'd am.

To loose what once was mine
Would grieve me more
Then those inconstant sweets of thine
Had pleas'd my soul before.

Now I have not lost the blisse
I ne'r possest;
And spight of fate am blest in this,
That I was never blest.

Thomas Stanley.

To Celia *pleading want of Merit.*

DEar urge no more that killing cause
Of our divorce;
Love is not fetter'd by such laws,
Nor bows to any force:
Though thou deniest I should be thine,
Yet say not thou deserv'st not to be mine.

Oh rather frown away my breath
With thy disdain,
Or flatter me with smiles to death;
By joy or sorrow slain,
'Tis lesse crime to be kill'd by thee,
Then I thus cause of mine own death should be.

Thy self of beauty to devest
And me of love,
Or from the worth of thine own breast
Thus to detract, would prove
In us a blindnesse, and in thee
At best a sacrilegious modestie.

But (*Celia*) if thou wilt despise
What all admire,
Nor rate thy self at the just price
Of beauty or desire,
Yet meet my flames and thou shalt see
That equal love knows no disparity.

Thomas Stanley.

La Belle Confidente.

YOu earthly Souls that court a wanton flame,
Whose pale weak influence
Can rise no higher then the humble name
And narrow laws of Sence,
Learn by our friendship to create
An immaterial fire,
Whose brightnesse Angels may admire,
But cannot emulate.

Sicknesse may fright the roses from her cheek,
Or make the Lilies fade,
But all the subtile wayes that death doth seek
Cannot my love invade:
Flames that are kindled by the eye,
Through time and age expire;
But ours that boast a reach far higher
Can nor decay, nor die.

For when we must resign our vital breath,
Our Loves by Fate benighted,
We by this friendship shall survive in death,
Even in divorce united.
Weak Love through fortune or distrust
In time forgets to burn,
But this pursues us to the Urn,
And marries either's Dust.

Thomas Stanley.

The Divorce.

DEar, back my wounded heart restore,
And turn away thy powerful eyes,
Flatter my willing soul no more,
Love must not hope what Fate denies.

Take, take away thy smiles and kisses,
Thy Love wounds deeper then Disdain,
For he that sees the Heaven he misses,
Sustains two Hels, of losse and pain.

Shouldst thou some others suit prefer,
I might return thy scorn to thee,
And learn Apostasie of her
Who taught me first Idolatry.

Or in thy unrelenting breast
Should I disdain or coynesse move,
He by thy hate might be releas't,
Who now is prisoner to thy love.

Since then unkind Fate will divorce
Those whom Affection long united,
Be thou as cruel as this force,
And I in death shall be delighted.

Thus whilst so many suppliants woe
And beg they may thy pitty prove,
I onely for thy scorn do sue,
'Tis charity here not to love.

Thomas Stanley.

The Exequies.

DRaw neer
You Lovers that complain
Of Fortune or Disdain,
And to my Ashes lend a tear;
Melt the hard marble with your grones.
And soften the relentlesse Stones,
Whose cold imbraces the sad Subject hide
Of all Loves cruelties, and Beauties Pride.

No Verse
No Epicedium bring,
Nor peaceful Requiem sing,
To charm the terrours of my Herse;
No prophane Numbers must flow neer
The sacred silence that dwells here;
Vast Griefs are dumb, softly, oh softly mourn
Lest you disturb the Peace attends my Urn.

Yet strew
Upon my dismall Grave,
Such offerings as you have,
Forsaken Cypresse and sad Ewe;
For kinder Flowers can take no Birth
Or growth from such unhappy Earth.
Weep only o're my Dust, and say, Here lies
To Love and Fate an equal Sacrifice.

Thomas Stanley.

Sonnet.

TEll me no more how fair she is,
I have no minde to hear
The story of that distant bliss
I never shall come near:
By sad experience I have found
That her perfection is my wound.

And tell me not how fond I am
To tempt a daring Fate,
From whence no triumph ever came,
But to repent too late:
There is some hope ere long I may
In silence dote my self away.

I ask no pity (Love) from thee,
Nor will thy justice blame,
So that thou wilt not envy mee
The glory of my flame:
Which crowns my heart when ere it dyes,
In that it falls her sacrifice.

Henry King.

The Spring.

THough you be absent here, I needs must say
The *Trees* as beauteous are, and *flowers* as gay,
As ever they were wont to be;
Nay the *Birds* rural musick too
Is as melodious and free,
As if they sung to pleasure you:
I saw a *Rose-Bud* o'pe this morn; I'll swear
The blushing *Morning* open'd not more fair.

How could it be so fair, and you away?
How could the *Trees* be beauteous, *Flowers* so gay?
Could they remember but last year,
How *you* did *Them*, *They you* delight,
The sprouting leaves which saw you here,
And call'd their *Fellows* to the sight,
Would, looking round for the same sight in vain,
Creep back into their silent *Barks* again.

Where ere you walk'd trees were as reverend made,
As when of old *Gods* dwelt in every shade.
Is't possible they should not know,
What loss of honor they sustain,
That thus they smile and flourish now,
And still their former pride retain?
Dull *Creatures!* 'tis not without Cause that she,
Who fled the *God of wit*, was made a *Tree*.

In ancient times sure they much wiser were,
When they rejoyc'd the *Thracian* verse to hear;
In vain did *Nature* bid them stay,
When *Orpheus* had his song begun,
They call'd their wondring *roots* away,
And bad them silent to him run.
How would those learned trees have followed you?
You would have drawn *Them*, and their *Poet* too.

But who can blame them now? for, since you're gone,
They're here the *only Fair*, and *Shine alone*.
You did their *Natural Rights* invade;
Where ever you did walk or sit,
The thickest Boughs could make no *shade*,
Although the Sun had granted it:
The fairest *Flowers* could please no more, neer you,
Then *Painted Flowers*, set next to them, could do.

When e're then you come hither, that shall be
The time, which this to others is, to *Me.*
The little joys which here are now,
The name of Punishments do bear;
When by their sight they let us know
How we depriv'd of greater are.
'Tis you the best of *Seasons* with you bring;
This is for *Beasts*, and that for *Men* the *Spring.*

Abraham Cowley.

The Change.

LOve in her Sunny Eyes does basking play;
Love walks the pleasant Mazes of her Hair;
Love does on both her Lips for ever stray;
And *sows* and *reaps* a thousand *kisses* there.
In all her outward parts *Love* 's always seen;
But, oh, He never went within.

Within *Love's* foes, his greatest foes abide,
Malice, Inconstancy, and Pride.
So the Earths face, Trees, Herbs, and Flowers do dress,
With other beauties numberless:
But at the *Center*, *Darkness* is, and *Hell*;
There wicked *Spirits*, and there the *Damned* dwell.

With me alas, quite contrary it fares;
Darkness and *Death* lies in my weeping eyes,
Despair and Paleness in my face appears,
And Grief, and Fear, Love's greatest Enemies;
But, like the *Persian-Tyrant*, *Love* within
Keeps his proud *Court*, and ne're is seen.

Oh take *my Heart*, and by that means you'll prove
Within too stor'd enough of *Love*:
Give me but Yours, I'll by that change so thrive,
That *Love* in all my parts shall live.
So powerful is this change, it render can,
My *outside Woman*, and your *inside Man*.

Abraham Cowley.

To his Coy Mistress.

HAd we but World enough, and Time,
This coyness Lady were no crime.
We would sit down, and think which way
To walk, and pass our long Loves Day.
Thou by the *Indian Ganges* side
Should'st Rubies find: I by the Tide
Of *Humber* would complain. I would
Love you ten years before the Flood:
And you should if you please refuse
Till the Conversion of the *Jews*.
My vegetable Love should grow
Vaster then Empires, and more slow.
An hundred years should go to praise
Thine Eyes, and on thy Forehead Gaze.
Two hundred to adore each Breast:
But thirty thousand to the rest.
An Age at least to every part,
And the last Age should show your Heart.
For Lady you deserve this State;
Nor would I love at lower rate.

But at my back I alwaies hear
Times winged Charriot hurrying near:
And yonder all before us lye
Desarts of vast Eternity.
Thy Beauty shall no more be found;
Nor, in thy marble Vault, shall sound
My ecchoing Song: then Worms shall try
That long preserv'd Virginity:
And your quaint Honour turn to dust;
And into ashes all my Lust.
The Grave's a fine and private place,
But none I think do there embrace.
Now therefore, while the youthful hew
Sits on thy skin like morning ⟨dew⟩
And while thy willing Soul transpires
At every pore with instant Fires,
Now let us sport us while we may;
And now, like am'rous birds of prey,
Rather at once our Time devour,
Than languish in his slow-chapt pow'r.
Let us roll all our Strength, and all
Our sweetness, up into one Ball:
And tear our Pleasures with rough strife,
Thorough the Iron gates of Life.
Thus, though we cannot make our Sun
Stand still, yet we will make him run.

Andrew Marvell.

The Gallery.

CLora come view my Soul, and tell
Whether I have contriv'd it well.
Now all its several lodgings lye
Compos'd into one Gallery;
And the great *Arras*-hangings, made
Of various Faces, by are laid;
That, for all furniture, you'l find
Only your Picture in my Mind.

Here Thou art painted in the Dress
Of an Inhumane Murtheress;
Examining upon our Hearts
Thy fertile Shop of cruel Arts:
Engines more keen than ever yet
Adorned Tyrants Cabinet;
Of which the most tormenting are
Black Eyes, red Lips, and curled Hair.

But, on the other side, th'art drawn
Like to *Aurora* in the Dawn;
When in the East she slumb'ring lyes,
And stretches out her milky Thighs;
While all the morning Quire does sing,
And *Manna* falls, and Roses spring;
And, at thy Feet, the wooing Doves
Sit perfecting their harmless Loves.

Like an Enchantress here thou show'st,
Vexing thy restless Lover's Ghost;
And, by a Light obscure, dost rave
Over his Entrails, in the Cave;

Divining thence, with horrid Care,
How long thou shalt continue fair;
And (when inform'd) them throw'st away,
To be the greedy Vultur's prey.

But, against that, thou sit'st a float
Like *Venus* in her pearly Boat.
The *Halcyons*, calming all that's nigh,
Betwixt the Air and Water fly.
Or, if some rowling Wave appears,
A Mass of Ambergris it bears.
Nor blows more Wind than what may well
Convoy the Perfume to the Smell.

These Pictures and a thousand more,
Of Thee, my Gallery does store;
In all the Forms thou can'st invent,
Either to please me, or torment:
For thou alone to people me,
Art grown a num'rous Colony;
And a Collection choicer far
Then or *White-hall*'s, or *Mantua*'s were.

But, of these Pictures and the rest,
That at the Entrance likes me best:
Where the same Posture, and the Look
Remains, with which I first was took.
A tender Shepherdess, whose Hair
Hangs loosely playing in the Air,
Transplanting Flow'rs from the green Hill,
To crown her Head, and Bosome fill.

Andrew Marvell.

The Fair Singer.

TO make a final conquest of all me,
Love did compose so sweet an Enemy,
In whom both Beauties to my death agree,
Joyning themselves in fatal Harmony;
That while she with her Eyes my Heart does bind,
She with her Voice might captivate my Mind.

I could have fled from One but singly fair:
My dis-intangled Soul it self might save,
Breaking the curled trammels of her hair.
But how should I avoid to be her Slave,
Whose subtile Art invisibly can wreath
My Fetters of the very Air I breath?

It had been easie fighting in some plain,
Where Victory might hang in equal choice.
But all resistance against her is vain,
Who has th' advantage both of Eyes and Voice.
And all my Forces needs must be undone,
She having gained both the Wind and Sun.

Andrew Marvell.

The Definition of Love.

MY Love is of a birth as rare
As 'tis for object strange and high:
It was begotten by despair
Upon Impossibility.

Magnanimous Despair alone
Could show me so divine a thing,
Where feeble Hope could ne'r have flown
But vainly flapt its Tinsel Wing.

And yet I quickly might arrive
Where my extended Soul is fixt,
But Fate does Iron wedges drive,
And alwaies crouds it self betwixt.

For Fate with jealous Eye does see
Two perfect Loves; nor lets them close:
Their union would her ruine be,
And her Tyrannick pow'r depose.

And therefore her Decrees of Steel
Us as the distant Poles have plac'd,
(Though Loves whole World on us doth wheel)
Not by themselves to be embrac'd.

Unless the giddy Heaven fall,
And Earth some new Convulsion tear;
And, us to joyn, the World should all
Be cramp'd into a *Planisphere*.

As Lines so Loves *oblique* may well
Themselves in every Angle greet:
But ours so truly *Paralel*,
Though infinite can never meet.

Therefore the Love which us doth bind,
But Fate so enviously debarrs,
Is the Conjunction of the Mind,
And Opposition of the Stars.

Andrew Marvell.

The Picture of little T. C. *in a Prospect of Flowers.*

SEe with what simplicity
This Nimph begins her golden daies!
In the green Grass she loves to lie,
And there with her fair Aspect tames
The Wilder Flow'rs, and gives them names:
But only with the Roses playes;
And them does tell
What Colour best becomes them, and what Smell.

Who can foretel for what high cause
This Darling of the Gods was born!
Yet this is She whose chaster Laws
The wanton Love shall one day fear,
And, under her command severe,
See his Bow broke and Ensigns torn.
Happy, who can
Appease this virtuous Enemy of Man!

O then let me in time compound,
And parly with those conquering Eyes;
Ere they have try'd their force to wound,
Ere, with their glancing wheels, they drive
In Triumph over Hearts that strive,
And them that yield but more despise.
Let me be laid,
Where I may see thy Glories from some Shade.

Mean time, whilst every verdant thing
It self does at thy Beauty charm,
Reform the errours of the Spring;
Make that the Tulips may have share
Of sweetness, seeing they are fair;
And Roses of their thorns disarm:
But most procure
That Violets may a longer Age endure.

But O young beauty of the Woods,
Whom Nature courts with fruits and flow'rs,
Gather the Flow'rs, but spare the Buds;
Lest *Flora* angry at thy crime,
To kill her Infants in their prime,
Do quickly make th' Example Yours;
And, ere we see,
Nip in the blossome all our hopes and Thee.

Andrew Marvell.

To my Excellent Lucasia, *on our Friendship.*

I Did not live until this time
Crown'd my felicity,
When I could say without a crime,
I am not thine, but Thee.

This Carcass breath'd, and walkt, and slept,
So that the World believ'd
There was a Soul the Motions kept;
But they were all deceiv'd.

For as a Watch by art is wound
  To motion, such was mine:
But never had *Orinda* found
  A Soul till she found thine;

Which now inspires, cures and supplies,
  And guides my darkned Breast:
For thou art all that I can prize,
  My Joy, my Life, my Rest.

No Bridegrooms nor Crown-conquerors mirth
  To mine compar'd can be:
They have but pieces of this Earth,
  I've all the World in thee.

Then let our Flames still light and shine,
  And no false fear controul,
As innocent as our Design,
  Immortal as our Soul.

Katherine Philips.

To my Lucasia, *in defence of declared Friendship.*

O My *Lucasia*, let us speak our Love,
  And think not that impertinent can be,
Which to us both doth such assurance prove,
  And whence we find how justly we agree.

Before we knew the treasures of our Love,
  Our noble aims our joys did entertain;
And shall enjoyment nothing then improve?
  'Twere best for us then to begin again.

Now we have gain'd, we must not stop, and sleep
Out all the rest of our mysterious reign:
It is as hard and glorious to keep
A victory, as it is to obtain.

Nay to what end did we once barter Minds,
Only to know and to neglect the claim?
Or (like some Wantons) our Pride pleasure finds
To throw away the thing at which we aim.

If this be all our Friendship does design,
We covet not enjoyment then, but power:
To our Opinion we our Bliss confine,
And love to have, but not to smell, the flower.

Ah! then let Misers bury thus their Gold,
Who though they starve, no farthing will produce:
But we lov'd to enjoy and to behold,
And sure we cannot spend our stock by use.

Think not 'tis needless to repeat desires;
The fervent Turtles alwaies court and bill,
And yet their spotless passion never tires,
But does increase by repetition still.

Although we know we love, yet while our Soul
Is thus imprison'd by the Flesh we wear,
There's no way left that bondage to controul,
But to convey transactions through the Ear.

Nay, though we read our passions in the Eye,
It will oblige and please to tell them too:
Such joys as these by motion multiply,
Were't but to find that our Souls told us true.

Believe not then, that being now secure
  Of either's heart, we have no more to do:
The Spheres themselves by motion do endure,
  And they move on by Circulation too.

And as a River, when it once hath paid
  The tribute which it to the Ocean owes,
Stops not, but turns, and having curl'd and play'd
  On its own waves, the shore it overflows:

So the Soul's motion does not end in bliss,
  But on her self she scatters and dilates,
And on the Object doubles till by this
  She finds new joys which that reflux creates.

But then because it cannot all contain,
  It seeks a vent by telling the glad news,
First to the Heart which did its joys obtain,
  Then to the Heart which did those joys produce.

When my Soul then doth such excursions make,
  Unless thy Soul delight to meet it too,
What satisfaction can it give or take,
  Thou being absent at the interview?

'Tis not Distrust; for were that plea allow'd,
  Letters and Visits all would useless grow:
Love's whole expression then would be its cloud,
  And it would be refin'd to nothing so.

If I distrust, 'tis my own worth for thee,
  'Tis my own fitness for a love like thine;
And therefore still new evidence would see,
  T'assure my wonder that thou canst be mine.

But as the Morning-Sun to drooping Flowers,
  As weary Travellers a Shade do find,
As to the parched Violet Evening-showers;
  Such is from thee to me a Look that's kind.

But when that Look is drest in Words, 'tis like
  The mystick pow'r of Musick's unison;
Which when the finger doth one Viol strike,
  The other's string heaves to reflection.

Be kind to me, and just then to our love,
  To which we owe our free and dear Converse;
And let not tract of Time wear or remove
  It from the privilege of that Commerce.

Tyrants do banish what they can't requite:
  But let us never know such mean desires;
But to be grateful to that Love delight
  Which all our joys and noble thoughts inspires.

Katherine Philips.

DIVINE POEMS.

Holy Sonnets.

THou hast made me, And shall thy worke decay?
Repaire me now, for now mine end doth haste,
I runne to death, and death meets me as fast,
And all my pleasures are like yesterday;
I dare not move my dimme eyes any way,
Despaire behind, and death before doth cast
Such terrour, and my feeble flesh doth waste
By sinne in it, which it t'wards hell doth weigh;
Onely thou art above, and when towards thee
By thy leave I can looke, I rise againe;
But our old subtle foe so tempteth me,
That not one houre my selfe I can sustaine;
Thy Grace may wing me to prevent his art,
And thou like Adamant draw mine iron heart.

THis is my playes last scene, here heavens appoint
My pilgrimages last mile; and my race
Idly, yet quickly runne, hath this last pace,
My spans last inch, my minutes latest point,
And gluttonous death, will instantly unjoynt
My body, and soule, and I shall sleepe a space,
But my'ever-waking part shall see that face,
Whose feare already shakes my every joynt:
Then, as my soule, to'heaven her first seate, takes flight,
And earth-borne body, in the earth shall dwell,
So, fall my sinnes, that all may have their right,
To where they'are bred, and would presse me, to hell.
Impute me righteous, thus purg'd of evill,
For thus I leave the world, the flesh, the devill.

AT the round earths imagin'd corners, blow
Your trumpets, Angells, and arise, arise
From death, you numberlesse infinities
Of soules, and to your scattred bodies goe,
All whom the flood did, and fire shall o'erthrow,
All whom warre, dearth, age, agues, tyrannies,
Despaire, law, chance, hath slaine, and you whose eyes,
Shall behold God, and never tast deaths woe.
But let them sleepe, Lord, and mee mourne a space,
For, if above all these, my sinnes abound,
'Tis late to aske abundance of thy grace,
When wee are there; here on this lowly ground,
Teach mee how to repent; for that's as good
As if thou'hadst seal'd my pardon, with thy blood.

DEath be not proud, though some have called thee
Mighty and dreadfull, for, thou art not so,
For, those, whom thou think'st, thou dost overthrow,
Die not, poore death, nor yet canst thou kill me.
From rest and sleepe, which but thy pictures bee,
Much pleasure, then from thee, much more must flow,
And soonest our best men with thee doe goe,
Rest of their bones, and soules deliverie.
Thou art slave to Fate, Chance, kings, and desperate men,
And dost with poyson, warre, and sicknesse dwell,
And poppie, or charmes can make us sleepe as well,
And better then thy stroake; why swell'st thou then;
One short sleepe past, wee wake eternally,
And death shall be no more; death, thou shalt die.

WHat if this present were the worlds last night?
Marke in my heart, O Soule, where thou dost dwell,
The picture of Christ crucified, and tell
Whether that countenance can thee affright,
Teares in his eyes quench the amasing light,
Blood fills his frownes, which from his pierc'd head fell.
And can that tongue adjudge thee unto hell,
Which pray'd forgivenesse for his foes fierce spight?
No, no; but as in my idolatrie
I said to all my profane mistresses,
Beauty, of pitty, foulnesse onely is
A signe of rigour: so I say to thee,
To wicked spirits are horrid shapes assign'd,
This beauteous forme assures a pitious minde.

BAtter my heart, three person'd God; for, you
As yet but knocke, breathe, shine, and seeke to mend;
That I may rise, and stand, o'erthrow mee,'and bend
Your force, to breake, blowe, burn and make me new.
I, like an usurpt towne, to'another due,
Labour to'admit you, but Oh, to no end,
Reason your viceroy in mee, mee should defend,
But is captiv'd, and proves weake or untrue.
Yet dearely'I love you,'and would be loved faine,
But am betroth'd unto your enemie:
Divorce mee,'untie, or breake that knot againe;
Take mee to you, imprison mee, for I
Except you'enthrall mee, never shall be free,
Nor ever chast, except you ravish mee.

SHow me deare Christ, thy spouse, so bright and clear.
What! is it She, which on the other shore
Goes richly painted? or which rob'd and tore
Laments and mournes in Germany and here?
Sleepes she a thousand, then peepes up one yeare?
Is she selfe truth and errs? now new, now outwore?
Doth she, and did she, and shall she evermore
On one, on seaven, or on no hill appeare?
Dwells she with us, or like adventuring knights
First travaile we to seeke and then make Love?
Betray kind husband thy spouse to our sights
And let myne amorous soule court thy mild Dove,
Who is most trew, and pleasing to thee, then
When she'is embrac'd and open to most men.

John Donne.

Goodfriday, 1613. *Riding Westward.*

LEt mans Soule be a Spheare, and then, in this,
The intelligence that moves, devotion is,
And as the other Spheares, by being growne
Subject to forraigne motions, lose their owne,
And being by others hurried every day,
Scarce in a yeare their naturall forme obey:
Pleasure or business, so, our Soules admit
For their first mover, and are whirld by it.
Hence is't, that I am carryed towards the West
This day, when my Soules forme bends toward the East.
There I should see a Sunne, by rising set,
And by that setting endlesse day beget;
But that Christ on this Crosse, did rise and fall,
Sinne had eternally benighted all.
Yet dare I'almost be glad, I do not see
That spectacle of too much weight for mee.
Who sees Gods face, that is selfe life, must dye;
What a death were it then to see God dye?
It made his owne Lieutenant Nature shrinke,
It made his footstoole crack, and the Sunne winke.
Could I behold those hands which span the Poles,
And turne all spheares at once, peirc'd with those holes?
Could I behold that endlesse height which is
Zenith to us, and our Antipodes,
Humbled below us? or that blood which is
The seat of all our Soules, if not of his,
Made durt of dust, or that flesh which was worne
By God, for his apparell, rag'd, and torne?
If on these things I durst not looke, durst I
Upon his miserable mother cast mine eye,

Who was Gods partner here, and furnish'd thus
Halfe of that Sacrifice, which ransom'd us?
Though these things, as I ride, be from mine eye,
They'are present yet unto my memory,
For that looks towards them; and thou look'st towards mee,
O Saviour, as thou hang'st upon the tree;
I turne my backe to thee, but to receive
Corrections, till thy mercies bid thee leave.
O thinke mee worth thine anger, punish mee,
Burne off my rusts, and my deformity,
Restore thine Image, so much, by thy grace,
That thou may'st know mee, and I'll turne my face.

John Donne.

A Hymne to CHRIST, *at the Authors last going into* Germany.

IN what torne ship soever I embarke,
That ship shall be my embleme of thy Arke;
What sea soever swallow mee, that flood
Shall be to mee an embleme of thy blood;
Though thou with clouds of anger do disguise
Thy face; yet through that maske I know those eyes,
Which, though they turne away sometimes,
They never will despise.

I sacrifice this Iland unto thee,
And all whom I lov'd there, and who lov'd mee;
When I have put our seas twixt them and mee,
Put thou thy sea betwixt my sinnes and thee.

As the trees sap doth seeke the root below
In winter, in my winter now I goe,
  Where none but thee, th'Eternall root
    Of true Love I may know.

Nor thou nor thy religion dost controule,
The amorousnesse of an harmonious Soule,
But thou would'st have that love thy selfe: As thou
Art jealous, Lord, so I am jealous now,
Thou lov'st not, till from loving more, thou free
My soule: Who ever gives, takes libertie:
  O, if thou car'st not whom I love
    Alas, thou lov'st not mee.

Seale then this bill of my Divorce to All,
On whom those fainter beames of love did fall;
Marry those loves, which in youth scattered bee
On Fame, Wit, Hopes (false mistresses) to thee.
Churches are best for Prayer, that have least light:
To see God only, I goe out of sight:
  And to scape stormy dayes, I chuse
    An Everlasting night.

John Donne.

Hymne to GOD *my* GOD, *in my sicknesse.*

SInce I am comming to that Holy roome,
  Where, with thy Quire of Saints for evermore,
I shall be made thy Musique; As I come
  I tune the Instrument here at the dore,
  And what I must doe then, thinke here before.

Whilst my Physitians by their love are growne
  Cosmographers, and I their Mapp, who lie
Flat on this bed, that by them may be showne
  That this is my South-west discoverie
  Per fretum febris, by these streights to die,

I joy, that in these straits, I see my West;
  For, though theire currants yeeld returne to none,
What shall my West hurt me? As West and East
  In all flatt Maps (and I am one) are one,
  So death doth touch the Resurrection.

Is the Pacifique Sea my home? Or are
  The Easterne riches? Is *Ierusalem*?
Anyan, and *Magellan*, and *Gibraltare*,
  All streights, and none but streights, are wayes to them,
  Whether where *Iaphet* dwelt, or *Cham*, or *Sem*.

We thinke that *Paradise* and *Calvarie*,
  Christs Crosse, and *Adams* tree, stood in one place;
Looke Lord, and finde both *Adams* met in me;
  As the first *Adams* sweat surrounds my face,
  May the last *Adams* blood my soule embrace.

So, in his purple wrapp'd receive mee Lord,
  By these his thornes give me his other Crowne;
And as to others soules I preach'd thy word,
  Be this my Text, my Sermon to mine owne,
  Therfore that he may raise the Lord throws down.

John Donne.

A Hymn to GOD THE FATHER.

WIlt thou forgive that sinn, where I begunn,
Which is my sinn, though it were done before?
Wilt thou forgive those sinns through which I runn
And doe run still, though still I doe deplore?
When thou has done, thou hast not done,
For, I have more.

Wilt thou forgive that sinn, by which I'have wonne
Others to sinn, and made my sinn their dore?
Wilt thou forgive that sinn which I did shunne
A yeare or twoe, but wallowed in a score?
When thou hast done, thou hast not done,
For I have more.

I have a sinn of feare that when I have spunn
My last thred, I shall perish on the shore;
Sweare by thy self that at my Death, thy Sonne
Shall shine as he shines nowe, & heretofore;
And having done that, thou hast done,
I feare noe more.

John Donne.

A Hymn to my GOD *in a night of my late Sicknesse*

OH thou great Power, in whom I move,
For whom I *live*, to whom I *die*,
Behold me through thy beams of *love*,
Whilest on this *Couch* of *tears* I lye;
And Cleanse my sordid *soul* within,
By thy *Christs Bloud*, the *bath* of sin.

No hallowed oyls, no grains I need,
No rags of Saints, no purging fire,
One rosie drop from *David's* Seed
Was worlds of seas, to quench thine Ire.
O pretious Ransome! which once paid,
That *Consummatum est* was said.

And said by *him*, that said no more,
But *seal'd* it with his sacred *breath*.
Thou then, that hast dispung'd my score,
And dying, wast the death of *death*;
Be to me now, on thee I call,
My Life, my Strength, my Joy, my All.

Sir Henry Wotton.

A Dialogue betwixt God *and the* Soul.

Imitatio Horatianae Odes 9 lib. 3 Donec gratus eram tibi

Soul. WHilst my *Souls* eye beheld no light
But what stream'd from thy gracious sight;
To me the worlds greatest King
Seem'd but some little vulgar thing.

God. Whilest thou prov'dst pure; and that in thee
I could glass al my Deity:
How glad did I from Heaven depart,
To find a Lodging in thy heart!

S. Now Fame and Greatness bear the sway,
('Tis they that hold my prisons Key:)
For whom my soul would dy, might shee
Leave them her Immortality.

G. I, and some few pure Souls conspire,
And burne both in a mutuall fire,
For whom I'ld dy once more, ere they
Should miss of Heavens eternal day.

S. But Lord! what if I turn againe,
And with an adamantine chain,
Lock me to thee? What if I chase
The world away to give thee place?

G. Then though these souls in whom I joy
Are *Seraphins*, Thou but a Toy,
A foolish Toy, yet once more I
Would with Thee live, and for thee die.

Ignoto.

On the morning of CHRISTS *Nativity.*

THis is the Month, and this the happy morn
Wherin the Son of Heav'ns eternal King,
Of wedded Maid, and Virgin Mother born,
Our great redemption from above did bring;
For so the holy sages once did sing,
That he our deadly forfeit should release,
And with his Father work us a perpetual peace.

That glorious Form, that Light unsufferable,
And that far-beaming blaze of Majesty,
Wherwith he wont at Heav'ns high Councel-Table,
To sit the midst of Trinal Unity,
He laid aside; and here with us to be,
Forsook the Courts of everlasting Day,
And chose with us a darksom House of mortal Clay.

Say Heav'nly Muse, shall not thy sacred vein
Afford a present to the Infant God?
Hast thou no vers, no hymn, or solemn strein,
To welcom him to this his new abode,
Now while the Heav'n by the Suns team untrod,
  Hath took no print of the approching light,
And all the spangled host keep watch in squadrons bright?

See how from far upon the Eastern rode
The Star-led Wisards haste with odours sweet:
O run, prevent them with thy humble ode,
And lay it lowly at his blessed feet;
Have thou the honour first, thy Lord to greet,
  And joyn thy voice unto the Angel Quire,
From out his secret Altar toucht with hallow'd fire.

The Hymn.

It was the Winter wilde,
While the Heav'n-born-childe,
  All meanly wrapt in the rude manger lies;
Nature in aw to him
Had doff't her gawdy trim,
  With her great Master so to sympathize:
It was no season then for her
To wanton with the Sun her lusty Paramour.

Onely with speeches fair
She woo's the gentle Air
  To hide her guilty front with innocent Snow,
And on her naked shame,
Pollute with sinfull blame,
  The Saintly Vail of Maiden white to throw,
Confounded, that her Makers eyes
Should look so neer upon her foul deformities.

But he her fears to cease,
Sent down the meek-eyd Peace,
  She crown'd with Olive green, came softly sliding
Down through the turning sphear
His ready Harbinger,
  With Turtle wing the amorous clouds dividing,
And waving wide her mirtle wand,
She strikes a universall Peace through Sea and Land.

No War, or Battails sound
Was heard the World around:
  The idle spear and shield were high up hung;
The hooked Chariot stood
Unstain'd with hostile blood,
  The Trumpet spake not to the armed throng,
And Kings sate still with awfull eye,
As if they surely knew their sovran Lord was by.

But peacefull was the night
Wherin the Prince of light
  His raign of peace upon the earth began:
The Windes with wonder whist,
Smoothly the waters kist,
  Whispering new joyes to the milde Ocean,
Who now hath quite forgot to rave,
While Birds of Calm sit brooding on the charmed wave.

The Stars with deep amaze
Stand fixt in stedfast gaze,
  Bending one way their pretious influence,
And will not take their flight,
For all the morning light,
  Or *Lucifer* that often warn'd them thence;
But in their glimmering Orbs did glow,
Untill their Lord himself bespake, and bid them go.

And though the shady gloom
Had given day her room,
The Sun himself with-held his wonted speed,
And hid his head for shame,
As his inferiour flame,
The new-enlightn'd world no more should need;
He saw a greater Sun appear
Then his bright Throne, or burning Axletree could bear.

The Shepherds on the Lawn,
Or ere the point of dawn,
Sate simply chatting in a rustick row;
Full little thought they than,
That the mighty *Pan*
Was kindly com to live with them below;
Perhaps their loves, or els their sheep,
Was all that did their silly thoughts so busie keep.

When such musick sweet
Their hearts and ears did greet,
As never was by mortall finger strook,
Divinely-warbled voice
Answering the stringed noise,
As all their souls in blisfull rapture took:
The Air such pleasure loth to lose,
With thousand echo's still prolongs each heav'nly close.

Nature that heard such sound
Beneath the hollow round
Of *Cynthia*'s seat, the Airy region thrilling,
Now was almost won
To think her part was don,
And that her raign had here its last fulfilling;
She knew such harmony alone
Could hold all Heav'n and Earth in happier union.

At last surrounds their sight
A Globe of circular light,
That with long beams the shame-fac't night array'd,
The helmed Cherubim
And sworded Seraphim,
Are seen in glittering ranks with wings displaid,
Harping in loud and solemn quire,
With unexpressive notes to Heav'ns new-born Heir.

Such Musick (as 'tis said)
Before was never made,
But when of old the sons of morning sung,
While the Creator Great
His constellations set,
And the well-ballanc't world on hinges hung,
And cast the dark foundations deep,
And bid the weltring waves their oozy channel keep.

Ring out ye Crystall sphears,
Once bless our human ears,
(If ye have power to touch our senses so)
And let your silver chime
Move in melodious time;
And let the Base of Heav'ns deep Organ blow,
And with your ninefold harmony
Make up full consort to th'Angelike symphony.

For if such holy Song
Enwrap our fancy long,
Time will run back, and fetch the age of gold,
And speckl'd vanity
Will sicken soon and die,
And leprous sin will melt from earthly mould,
And Hell it self will pass away,
And leave her dolorous mansions to the peering day.

Yea Truth, and Justice then
Will down return to men,
  Th'enameld *Arras* of the Rainbow wearing,
And Mercy set between,
Thron'd in Celestiall sheen,
  With radiant feet the tissued clouds down stearing,
And Heav'n as at som festivall,
Will open wide the Gates of her high Palace Hall.

But wisest Fate sayes no,
This must not yet be so,
  The Babe lies yet in smiling Infancy,
That on the bitter cross
Must redeem our loss;
  So both himself and us to glorifie:
Yet first to those ychain'd in sleep,
The wakefull trump of doom must thunder through the deep,

With such a horrid clang
As on mount *Sinai* rang
  While the red fire, and smouldring clouds out brake:
The aged Earth agast
With terrour of that blast,
  Shall from the surface to the center shake;
When at the worlds last session,
The dreadfull Judge in middle Air shall spread his throne.

And then at last our bliss
Full and perfect is,
  But now begins; for from this happy day
Th'old Dragon under ground
In straiter limits bound,
  Not half so far casts his usurped sway,
And wrath to see his Kingdom fail,
Swindges the scaly Horrour of his foulded tail.

The Oracles are dumm,
No voice or hideous humm
Runs through the arched roof in words deceiving.
Apollo from his shrine
Can no more divine,
With hollow shreik the steep of *Delphos* leaving.
No nightly trance, or breathed spell,
Inspires the pale-ey'd Priest from the prophetic cell.

The lonely mountains o're,
And the resounding shore,
A voice of weeping heard, and loud lament;
From haunted spring, and dale
Edg'd with poplar pale,
The parting Genius is with sighing sent,
With flowre-inwov'n tresses torn
The Nimphs in twilight shade of tangled thickets mourn.

In consecrated Earth,
And on the holy Hearth,
The *Lars*, and *Lemures* moan with midnight plaint,
In Urns, and Altars round,
A drear, and dying sound
Affrights the *Flamins* at their service quaint;
And the chill Marble seems to sweat,
While each peculiar power forgoes his wonted seat.

Peor, and *Baalim*,
Forsake their Temples dim,
With that twise-batter'd god of *Palestine*,
And mooned *Ashtaroth*,
Heav'ns Queen and Mother both,
Now sits not girt with Tapers holy shine,
The Libyc *Hammon* shrinks his horn,
In vain the *Tyrian* Maids their wounded *Thamuz* mourn.

And sullen *Moloch* fled,
Hath left in shadows dred,
His burning Idol all of blackest hue,
In vain with Cymbals ring,
They call the grisly king,
In dismall dance about the furnace blue;
The brutish gods of *Nile* as fast,
Isis and *Orus*, and the Dog *Anubis* hast.

Nor is *Osiris* seen
In *Memphian* Grove, or Green,
Trampling the unshowr'd Grasse with lowings loud:
Nor can he be at rest
Within his sacred chest,
Naught but profoundest Hell can be his shroud,
In vain with Timbrel'd Anthems dark
The sable-stoled Sorcerers bear his worshipt Ark.

He feels fròm *Juda*'s Land
The dredded Infants hand,
The rayes of *Bethlehem* blind his dusky eyn;
Nor all the gods beside,
Longer dare abide,
Not *Typhon* huge ending in snaky twine:
Our Babe to shew his Godhead true,
Can in his swadling bands controul the damned crew.

So when the Sun in bed,
Curtain'd with cloudy red,
Pillows his chin upon an Orient wave,
The flocking shadows pale,
Troop to th'infernall jail,
Each fetter'd Ghost slips to his severall grave,
And the yellow-skirted *Fayes*,
Fly after the Night-steeds, leaving their Moon-lov'd maze.

But see the Virgin blest,
Hath laid her Babe to rest.
Time is our tedious Song should here have ending,
Heav'ns youngest teemed Star,
Hath fixt her polisht Car,
Her sleeping Lord with Handmaid Lamp attending:
And all about the Courtly Stable,
Bright-harnest Angels sit in order serviceable.

John Milton.

Redemption.

HAving been tenant long to a rich Lord,
Not thriving, I resolved to be bold,
And make a suit unto him, to afford
A new small-rented lease, and cancell th' old.

In heaven at his manour I him sought:
They told me there, that he was lately gone
About some land, which he had dearly bought
Long since on earth, to take possession.

I straight return'd, and knowing his great birth,
Sought him accordingly in great resorts;
In cities, theatres, gardens, parks, and courts:
At length I heard a ragged noise and mirth

Of theeves and murderers: there I him espied,
Who straight, *Your suit is granted*, said, & died.

George Herbert.

Easter wings.

Lord, who createdst man in wealth and store,
Though foolishly he lost the same,
Decaying more and more,
Till he became
Most poore :
With thee
O let me rise
As larks, harmoniously,
And sing this day thy victories :
Then shall the fall further the flight in me.

My tender age in sorrow did beginne :
And still with sicknesses and shame
Thou didst so punish sinne,
That I became
Most thinne.
With thee
Let me combine,
And feel this day thy victorie :
For, if I imp my wing on thine,
Affliction shall advance the flight in me.

George Herbert.

Affliction.

WHen first thou didst entice to thee my heart,
I thought the service brave:
So many joyes I writ down for my part,
Besides what I might have
Out of my stock of naturall delights,
Augmented with thy gracious benefits.

I looked on thy furniture so fine,
And made it fine to me:
Thy glorious houshold-stuffe did me entwine,
And 'tice me unto thee;
Such starres I counted mine: both heav'n and earth
Payd me my wages in a world of mirth.

What pleasures could I want, whose King I served?
Where joyes my fellows were.
Thus argu'd into hopes, my thoughts reserved
No place for grief or fear.
Therefore my sudden soul caught at the place,
And made her youth and fiercenesse seek thy face

At first thou gav'st me milk and sweetnesses;
I had my wish and way:
My dayes were straw'd with flow'rs and happinesse;
There was no moneth but May.
But with my yeares sorrow did twist and grow,
And made a partie unawares for wo.

My flesh began unto my soul in pain,
Sicknesses cleave my bones;
Consuming agues dwell in ev'ry vein,
And tune my breath to grones.
Sorrow was all my soul; I scarce beleeved,
Till grief did tell me roundly, that I lived.

When I got health, thou took'st away my life,
And more; for my friends die:
My mirth and edge was lost; a blunted knife
Was of more use then I.
Thus thinne and lean without a fence or friend,
I was blown through with ev'ry storm and winde.

Whereas my birth and spirit rather took
The way that takes the town;
Thou didst betray me to a lingring book,
And wrap me in a gown.
I was entangled in the world of strife,
Before I had the power to change my life.

Yet, for I threatned oft the siege to raise,
Not simpring all mine age,
Thou often didst with Academick praise
Melt and dissolve my rage.
I took thy sweetned pill, till I came neare;
I could not go away, nor persevere.

Yet lest perchance I should too happie be
In my unhappinesse,
Turning my purge to food, thou throwest me
Into more sicknesses.
Thus doth thy power crosse-bias me, not making
Thine own gift good, yet me from my wayes taking.

Now I am here, what thou wilt do with me
None of my books will show:
I reade, and sigh, and wish I were a tree;
For sure then I should grow
To fruit or shade: at least some bird would trust
Her houshold to me, and I should be just.

Yet, though thou troublest me, I must be meek;
　　　　　　In weaknesse must be stout.
Well, I will change the service, and go seek
　　　　　　Some other master out.
Ah my deare God! though I am clean forgot,
Let me not love thee, if I love thee not.

George Herbert.

Jordan.

WHo sayes that fictions onely and false hair
　　Become a verse? Is there in truth no beautie?
Is all good structure in a winding stair?
May no lines passe, except they do their dutie
　　Not to a true, but painted chair?

Is it no verse, except enchanted groves
And sudden arbours shadow course-spunne lines?
Must purling streams refresh a lovers loves?
Must all be vail'd, while he that reades, divines,
　　Catching the sense at two removes?

Shepherds are honest people; let them sing:
Riddle who list, for me, and pull for Prime:
I envie no mans nightingale or spring;
Nor let them punish me with losse of ryme,
　　Who plainly say, *My God, My King.*

George Herbert.

The Church-floore.

MArk you the floore? that square & speckled stone,
Which looks so firm and strong,
Is *Patience*:

And th' other black and grave, wherewith each one
Is checker'd all along,
Humilitie:

The gentle rising, which on either hand
Leads to the Quire above,
Is *Confidence*:

But the sweet cement, which in one sure band
Ties the whole frame, is *Love*
And *Charitie*.

Hither sometimes Sinne steals, and stains
The marbles neat and curious veins:
But all is cleansed when the marble weeps.
Sometimes Death, puffing at the doore,
Blows all the dust about the floore:
But while he thinks to spoil the room, he sweeps.
Blest be the *Architect*, whose art
Could build so strong in a weak heart.

George Herbert.

The Windows.

LOrd, how can man preach thy eternall word?
He is a brittle crazie glasse:
Yet in thy temple thou dost him afford
This glorious and transcendent place,
To be a window, through thy grace.

But when thou dost anneal in glasse thy storie,
Making thy life to shine within
The holy Preachers ; then the light and glorie
More rev'rend grows, & more doth win ;
Which else shows watrish, bleak, & thin.

Doctrine and life, colours and light, in one
When they combine and mingle, bring
A strong regard and aw : but speech alone
Doth vanish like a flaring thing,
And in the eare, not conscience ring.

George Herbert.

Vertue.

SWeet day, so cool, so calm, so bright,
The bridall of the earth and skie :
The dew shall weep thy fall to night ;
For thou must die.

Sweet rose, whose hue angrie and brave
Bids the rash gazer wipe his eye :
Thy root is ever in its grave,
And thou must die.

Sweet spring, full of sweet dayes and roses,
A box where sweets compacted lie ;
My musick shows ye have your closes,
And all must die.

Onely a sweet and vertuous soul,
Like season'd timber, never gives;
But though the whole world turn to coal,
Then chiefly lives.

George Herbert.

Life.

I Made a posie, while the day ran by:
Here will I smell my remnant out, and tie
My life within this band.
But time did becken to the flowers, and they
By noon most cunningly did steal away,
And wither'd in my hand.

My hand was next to them, and then my heart:
I took, without more thinking, in good part
Times gentle admonition:
Who did so sweetly deaths sad taste convey,
Making my minde to smell my fatall day;
Yet sugring the suspicion.

Farewell deare flowers, sweetly your time ye spent,
Fit, while ye liv'd, for smell or ornament,
And after death for cures.
I follow straight without complaints or grief,
Since if my sent be good, I care not, if
It be as short as yours.

George Herbert.

JESU.

JESU is in my heart, his sacred name
Is deeply carved there: but th'other week
A great affliction broke the little frame,
Ev'n all to pieces: which I went to seek:
And first I found the corner, where was *J*,
After, where *ES*, and next where *U* was graved.
When I had got these parcels, instantly
I sat me down to spell them, and perceived
That to my broken heart he was *I ease you*,
And to my whole is *JESU.*

George Herbert.

The Collar.

I Struck the board, and cry'd, No more.
I will abroad.
What? shall I ever sigh and pine?
My lines and life are free; free as the rode,
Loose as the winde, as large as store.
Shall I be still in suit?
Have I no harvest but a thorn
To let me bloud, and not restore
What I have lost with cordiall fruit?
Sure there was wine
Before my sighs did drie it: there was corn
Before my tears did drown it.
Is the yeare onely lost to me?
Have I no bayes to crown it?

No flowers, no garlands gay? all blasted?
All wasted?
Not so, my heart: but there is fruit,
And thou hast hands.
Recover all thy sigh-blown age
On double pleasures: leave thy cold dispute
Of what is fit, and not; forsake thy cage,
Thy rope of sands,
Which pettie thoughts have made, and made to thee
Good cable, to enforce and draw,
And be thy law,
While thou didst wink and wouldst not see.
Away; take heed:
I will abroad.
Call in thy deaths head there: tie up thy fears.
He that forbears
To suit and serve his need,
Deserves his load.
But as I rav'd and grew more fierce and wilde
At every word,
Me thoughts I heard one calling, *Childe*:
And I reply'd, *My Lord*.

George Herbert.

Aaron.

HOlinesse on the head,
Light and perfections on the breast,
Harmonious bells below, raising the dead
To leade them unto life and rest.
Thus are true Aarons drest.

Profanenesse in my head,
Defects and darknesse in my breast,
A noise of passions ringing me for dead
Unto a place where is no rest.
Poore priest thus am I drest.

Onely another head
I have, another heart and breast,
Another musick, making live not dead,
Without whom I could have no rest:
In him I am well drest.

Christ is my onely head,
My alone onely heart and breast,
My onely musick, striking me ev'n dead;
That to the old man I may rest,
And be in him new drest.

So holy in my head,
Perfect and light in my deare breast,
My doctrine tun'd by Christ, (who is not dead,
But lives in me while I do rest)
Come people; Aaron's drest.

George Herbert.

Discipline.

THrow away thy rod,
Throw away thy wrath:
O my God,
Take the gentle path.

For my hearts desire
Unto thine is bent:
I aspire
To a full consent.

Not a word or look
I affect to own,
But by book,
And thy book alone.

Though I fail, I weep:
Though I halt in pace,
Yet I creep
To the throne of grace.

Then let wrath remove;
Love will do the deed:
For with love
Stonie hearts will bleed.

Love is swift of foot;
Love's a man of warre,
And can shoot,
And can hit from farre.

Who can scape his bow?
That which wrought on thee,
Brought thee low,
Needs must work on me.

Throw away thy rod;
Though man frailties hath,
Thou art God:
Throw away thy wrath.

George Herbert.

Love.

LOve bade me welcome: yet my soul drew back,
Guiltie of dust and sinne.
But quick-ey'd Love, observing me grow slack
From my first entrance in,
Drew nearer to me, sweetly questioning,
If I lack'd any thing.

A guest, I answer'd, worthy to be here:
Love said, you shall be he.
I the unkinde, ungratefull? Ah my deare,
I cannot look on thee.
Love took my hand, and smiling did reply,
Who made the eyes but I?

Truth Lord, but I have marr'd them: let my shame
Go where it doth deserve.
And know you not, sayes Love, who bore the blame?
My deare, then I will serve.
You must sit down, sayes Love, and taste my meat:
So I did sit and eat.

George Herbert.

Job XIII. XXIV.

Wherefore hidest thou thy face, and holdest me for thy enemie?

WHy dost thou shade thy lovely face? O why
Does that ecclipsing hand, so long, deny
The Sun-shine of thy soule-enliv'ning eye?

Without that *Light*, what light remaines in me?
Thou art my *Life*, my *Way*, my *Light*; in Thee
I live, I move, and by thy beames I see.

Thou art my *Life* ; If thou but turne away,
My life 's a thousand deaths : thou art my *Way* ;
Without thee, Lord, I travell not, but stray.

My *Light* thou art ; without thy glorious sight,
Mine eyes are darkned with perpetuall night.
My God, thou art my *Way*, my *Life*, my *Light*.

Thou art my *Way* ; I wander, if thou flie :
Thou art my *Light* ; If hid, how blind am I ?
Thou art my *Life* ; If thou withdraw, I die.

Mine eyes are blind and darke, I cannot see ;
To whom, or whither should my darknesse flee,
But to the *Light* ? And who 's that *Light* but Thee ?

My path is lost ; my wandring steps do stray ;
I cannot safely go, nor safely stay ;
Whom should I seek but Thee, my *Path*, my *Way* ?

O, I am dead : To whom shall I, poore I,
Repaire ? To whom shall my sad Ashes fly
But *Life* ? And where is *Life* but in thine eye ?

And yet thou turn'st away thy face, and fly'st me ;
And yet I sue for Grace, and thou deny'st me ;
Speake, art thou angry, Lord, or onely try'st me ?

Unskreene those heav'nly lamps, or tell me why
Thou shad'st thy face ; Perhaps, thou think'st, no eye
Can view those flames, and not drop downe and die.

If that be all, shine forth, and draw thee nigher ;
Let me behold and die ; for my desire
Is *Phœnix*-like to perish in that Fire.

Death-conquer'd *Laz'rus* was redeem'd by Thee;
If I am dead, Lord set deaths prisner free;
Am I more spent, or stink I worse than he?

If my pufft light be out, give leave to tine
My shamelesse snuffe at that bright *Lamp* of thine;
O what's thy *Light* the lesse for lighting mine?

If I have lost my Path, great Shepheard, say,
Shall I still wander in a doubtfull way?
Lord, shall a Lamb of *Isr'els* sheepfold stray?

Thou art the Pilgrims *Path*; the blind mans *Eye*;
The dead mans *Life*; on thee my hopes rely;
If thou remove, I erre; I grope; I die.

Disclose thy Sun-beames; close thy wings, and stay;
See see, how I am blind, and dead, and stray,
O thou, that art my *Light*, my *Life*, my *Way*.

Francis Quarles.

CANTICLES II. XVI.

My beloved is mine, and I am his; He feedeth among the Lillies.

EV'n like two little bank-dividing brookes,
That wash the pebles with their wanton streames,
And having rang'd and search'd a thousand nookes,
Meet both at lengthe in silver-brested *Thames*,
Where in a greater Current they conjoyne:
So I my Best-Beloveds am; so He is mine.

Ev'n so we met; and after long pursuit,
Ev'n so we joyn'd; we both became entire;
No need for either to renew a Suit,
For I was Flax and he was Flames of fire:
Our firm united soules did more than twine;
So I my Best-Beloveds am; so He is mine.

If all those glittring Monarchs that command
The servile Quarters of this earthly Ball,
Should tender, in Exchange, their shares of land,
I would not change my Fortunes for them all:
Their wealth is but a Counter to my Coyne;
The world's but theirs; but my Beloved's mine.

Nay, more; If the fair Thespian Ladies all
Should heap together their diviner treasure:
That Treasure should be deem'd a price too small
To buy a minutes Lease of half my Pleasure;
'Tis not the sacred wealth of all the Nine
Can buy my heart from Him; or His, from being mine.

Nor Time, nor Place, nor Chance, nor Death can bow
My least desires unto the least remove;
Hee's firmely mine by Oath; I, His, by Vow;
Hee's mine by Faith; and I am His by Love;
Hee's mine by Water; I am His, by Wine;
Thus I my Best-Beloveds am; Thus He is mine.

He is my Altar; I, his Holy Place;
I am his Guest; and he, my living Food;
I'm his, by Poenitence; He, mine by Grace;
I'm his, by Purchase; He is mine, by Blood;
Hee's my supporting Elme; and I, his Vine:
Thus I my Best-Beloveds am; Thus He is mine.

He gives me wealth; I give him all my Vowes:
I give him songs; He gives me length of dayes:
With wreathes of Grace he crownes my conqu'ring browes:
And I, his Temples, with a Crowne of Praise,
Which he accepts as an everlasting signe,
That I my Best-Beloveds am; that He is mine.

Francis Quarles.

Nox nocti indicat Scientiam. DAVID.

WHen I survay the bright
Cœlestiall spheare:
So rich with jewels hung, that night
Doth like an Æthiop bride appeare.

My soule her wings doth spread
And heaven-ward flies,
Th'Almighty's Mysteries to read
In the large volumes of the skies.

For the bright firmament
Shootes forth no flame
So silent, but is eloquent
In speaking the Creators name.

No unregarded star
Contracts its light
Into so small a Charactar,
Remov'd far from our humane sight:

But if we stedfast looke,
We shall discerne
In it as in some holy booke,
How man may heavenly knowledge learne.

It tells the Conqueror,
That farre-stretcht powre
Which his proud dangers traffique for,
Is but the triumph of an houre.

That from the farthest North,
Some Nation may
Yet undiscovered issue forth,
And ore his new got conquest sway.

Some Nation yet shut in
With hils of ice
May be let out to scourge his sinne
'Till they shall equall him in vice.

And then they likewise shall
Their ruine have,
For as your selves your Empires fall,
And every Kingdome hath a grave.

Thus those Cœlestiall fires,
Though seeming mute,
The fallacie of our desires
And all the pride of life confute.

For they have watcht since first
The World had birth:
And found sinne in it selfe accurst,
And nothing permanent on earth.

William Habington.

LOrd when the wise men came from farr
Ledd to thy Cradle by A Starr,
Then did the shepheards too rejoyce,
Instructed by thy Angells voyce,
Blest were the wisemen in their skill,
And shepheards in their harmelesse will.

Wisemen in tracing natures lawes
Ascend unto the highest cause,
Shepheards with humble fearefulnesse
Walke safely, though their light be lesse:
Though wisemen better know the way
It seemes noe honest heart can stray.

Ther is noe merrit in the wise
But love, (the shepheards sacrifice).
Wisemen all wayes of knowledge past,
To th' shepheards wonder come at last,
To know, can only wonder breede,
And not to know, is wonders seede.

A wiseman at the Alter bowes
And offers up his studied vowes
And is received; may not the teares,
Which spring too from a shepheards feares,
And sighs upon his fraylty spent,
Though not distinct, be eloquent?

Tis true, the object sanctifies
All passions which within us rise,
But since noe creature comprehends
The cause of causes, end of ends,
Hee who himselfe vouchsafes to know
Best pleases his creator soe.

When then our sorrowes we applye
To our owne wantes and poverty,
When wee looke up in all distresse
And our owne misery confesse
Sending both thankes and prayers above,
Then though wee do not know, we love.

Sidney Godolphin.

To the Noblest & Best of Ladyes, the Countesse of Denbigh,

Perswading her to Resolution in Religion.

WHat heav'n-intreated HEART is This
Stands trembling at the gate of blisse;
Holds fast the door, yet dares not venture
Fairly to open it, and enter,
Whose DEFINITION is a Doubt
Twixt Life & Death, twixt In & Out.
Say, lingring fair! why comes the birth
Of your brave soul so slowly forth?
Plead your pretences (o you strong
In weaknes!) why you choose so long
In labor of your selfe to ly,
Nor daring quite to live nor dy?
Ah linger not, lov'd soul! a slow
And late consent was a long No,
Who grants at last, a long time tryd
And did his best to have deny'd,
What magick bolts, what mystick Barres
Maintain the will in these strange warres!
What fatall, yet fantasick, bands
Keep The free Heart from it's own hands!

So when the year takes cold, we see
Poor waters their owne prisoners be.
Fetter'd, & lockt up fast they ly
In a sad selfe-captivity.
The' astonisht nymphs their flood's strange fate deplore,
To see themselves their own severer shore.
Thou that alone canst thaw this cold,
And fetch the heart from it's strong Hold;
Allmighty LOVE! end this long warr,
And of a meteor make a starr.
O fix this fair INDEFINITE.
And 'mongst thy shafts of soveraign light
Choose out that sure decisive dart
Which has the Key of this close heart,
Knowes all the corners of't, & can controul
The self-shutt cabinet of an unsearcht soul.
O let it be at last, love's houre.
Raise this tall Trophee of thy Powre;
Come once the conquering way; not to confute
But kill this rebell-word, IRRESOLUTE
That so, in spite of all this peevish strength
Of weaknes, she may write RESOLV'D AT LENGTH,
Unfold at length, unfold fair flowre
And use the season of love's showre,
Meet his well-meaning Wounds, wise heart!
And hast to drink the wholsome dart.
That healing shaft, which heavn till now
Hath in love's quiver hid for you.
O Dart of love! arrow of light!
O happy you, if it hitt right,
It must not fall in vain, it must
Not mark the dry regardles dust.
Fair one, it is your fate; and brings

Æternall worlds upon it's wings.
Meet it with wide-spread armes; & see
It's seat your soul's just center be.
Disband dull feares; give faith the day.
To save your life, kill your delay.
It is love's seege; and sure to be
Your triumph, though his victory.
'Tis cowardise that keeps this feild
And want of courage not to yeild.
Yeild then, ô yeild, that love may win
The Fort at last, and let life in.
Yeild quickly. Lest perhaps you prove
Death's prey, before the prize of love.
This Fort of your fair selfe, if't be not won,
He is repulst indeed; But you'are vndone.

Richard Crashaw.

Hymn of the Nativity.

Sung as by the Shepheards.

Chorus.

COme we shepheards whose blest Sight
Hath mett love's Noon in Nature's night;
Come lift we up our loftyer Song
And wake the SUN that lyes too long.

To all our world of well-stoln joy
He slept; and dream't of no such thing;
While we found out Heavn's fairer eye
And Kis't the Cradle of our KING.
Tell him He rises now too late
To show us ought worth looking at.

Tell him we now can show Him more
Then He e're show'd to mortall Sight;
Then he Himselfe e're saw before;
Which to be seen needes not His light.
Tell him, Tityrus, where th' hast been,
Tell him, Thyrsis, what th' hast seen.

Tityrus. Gloomy night embrac't the Place
Where The Noble Infant lay.
The Babe look't up & shew'd his Face;
In spite of Darknes, it was Day.
It was Thy day, Sweet! & did rise
Not from the East, but from thine Eyes.

Chorus. It was Thy day, Sweet, &c.

Thyrs. Winter chidde aloud; & sent
The angry North to wage his warres.
The North forgott his feirce Intent;
And left perfumes in stead of scarres.
By those sweet eyes persuasive powrs
Where he mean't frost, he scatter'd flowrs.

Chorus. By those sweet eyes, &c.

Both. We saw thee in thy baulmy Nest,
Young dawn of our æternall Day!
We saw thine eyes break from their Easte
And chase the trembling shades away.
We saw thee; & we blest the sight,
We saw thee by thine own sweet light.

Tity. Poor World (said I) what wilt thou doe
To entertain this starry Stranger ?
Is this the best thou canst bestow ?
A cold, and not too cleanly, manger ?
Contend ye powres of heav'n & earth
To fitt à bed for this huge birthe.

Cho. Contend ye powers, &c.

Thyr. Proud world, said I ; cease your contest,
And let the Mighty Babe alone.
The Phænix builds the Phænix' nest.
Lov's architecture is his own.
The Babe whose birth embraves this morn,
Made his own bed e're he was born.

Cho. The Babe whose, &c.

Tit. I saw the curl'd drops, soft & slow,
Come hovering o're the place's head ;
Offring their whitest sheets of snow
To furnish the fair Infant's bed :
Forbear, said I ; be not too bold.
Your fleece is white, But t'is too cold.

Cho. Forbear, sayd I, &c.

Thyr. I saw the obsequious Seraphins
Their rosy fleece of fire bestow,
For well they now can spare their wings,
Since Heavn it self lyes here below.
Well done, said I : but are you sure
Your down so warm, will passe for pure ?

Cho. Well done sayd I, &c.

Tit. No no, your KING's not yet to seeke
Where to repose his Royall HEAD,
See see, how soon his new-bloom'd CHEEK
Twixt's mother's brests is gone to bed.
Sweet choise, said we! no way but so
Not to ly cold, yet sleep in snow.

Cho. Sweet choise, said we, &c.

Both. We saw thee in thy baulmy nest,
Bright dawn of our æternall Day!
We saw thine eyes break from thir EAST
And chase the trembling shades away.
We saw thee: & we blest the sight.
We saw thee, by thine own sweet light.

Cho. We saw thee, &c.

Full Chorus.

Wellcome, all WONDERS in one sight!
Æternity shutt in a span.
Sommer in Winter. Day in Night.
Heaven in earth, & GOD in MAN.
Great little one! whose all-embracing birth
Lifts earth to heaven, stoopes heav'n to earth.

WELLCOME. Though nor to gold nor silk.
To more then Cæsar's birth right is;
Two sister-seas of Virgin-Milk,
With many a rarely-temper'd kisse
That breathes at once both MAID & MOTHER,
Warmes in the one, cooles in the other.

WELLCOME, though not to those gay flyes
Guilded ith' Beames of earthly kings;
Slippery soules in smiling eyes;
But to poor Shepherds, home-spun things:
Whose Wealth 's their flock; whose witt, to be
Well read in their simplicity.

Yet when young April's husband showrs
Shall blesse the fruitfull Maia's bed,
We'l bring the First-born of her flowrs
To kisse thy FEET & crown thy HEAD.
To thee, dread Lamb! whose love must keep
The shepheards, more then they the sheep.

To THEE, meek Majesty! soft KING
Of simple GRACES & sweet LOVES.
Each of us his lamb will bring
Each his pair of sylver Doves;
Till burnt at last in fire of Thy fair eyes,
Our selves become our own best SACRIFICE.

Richard Crashaw.

Hymn in Adoration of the Blessed Sacrament.

Adoro te.

WIth all the powres my poor Heart hath
Of humble love & loyall Faith,
Thus lowe (my hidden life!) I bow to thee
Whom too much love hath bow'd more low for me.
Down down, proud sense! Discourses dy!
Keep close, my soul's inquiring ey!
Nor touch nor tast must look for more
But each sitt still in his own Dore.

Your ports are all superfluous here,
Save That which lets in faith, the eare.
Faith is my skill. Faith can beleive
As fast as love new lawes can give.
Faith is my force. Faith strength affords
To keep pace with those powrfull words.
And words more sure, more sweet, then they,
Love could not think, truth could not say.

O let thy wretch find that releife
Thou didst afford the faithfull theife.
Plead for me, love! Alleage & show
That faith has farther, here, to goe,
And lesse to lean on. Because than
Though hidd as God, wounds writt thee man.
Thomas might touch; None but might see
At least the suffring side of thee;
And that too was thy self which thee did cover,
But here ev'n That's hid too which hides the other.

Sweet, consider then, that I
Though allow'd nor hand nor eye
To reach at thy lov'd Face; nor can
Tast thee God, or touch thee Man,
Both yet beleive; And wittnesse thee
My Lord too & my God, as lowd as He.

Help, lord, my Faith, my Hope increase;
And fill my portion in thy peace.
Give love for life; nor let my dayes
Grow, but in new powres to thy name & praise.

O dear memoriall of that Death
Which lives still, & allowes us breath!
Rich, Royall food! Bountyfull Bread!
Whose use denyes us to the dead;

Whose vitall gust alone can give
The same leave both to eat & live;
Live ever Bread of loves, & be
My life, my soul, my surer selfe to mee.

O soft self-wounding Pelican!
Whose brest weepes Balm for wounded man.
Ah this way bend thy benign floud
To'a bleeding Heart that gaspes for blood:
That blood, whose least drops soveraign be
To wash my worlds of sins from me.
Come love! Come LORD! & that long day
For which I languish, come away;
When this dry soul those eyes shall see,
And drink the unseal'd sourse of thee,
When Glory's sun faith's shades shall chase,
And for thy veil give me thy FACE.

AMEN.

Richard Crashaw.

Saint Mary Magdalene

or

The Weeper.

HAil, sister springs!
Parents of sylver-footed rills!
Ever bubling things!
Thawing crystall! snowy hills,
Still spending never spent! I mean
Thy fair eyes, sweet MAGDALENE!

Heavens thy fair eyes be;
Heavens of ever-falling starres.
'Tis seed-time still with thee
And starres thou sow'st, whose harvest dares
Promise the earth to counter shine
Whatever makes heavn's forhead fine.

But we'are deceived all.
Starres indeed they are too true;
For they but seem to fall,
As Heavn's other spangles doe.
It is not for our earth & us
To shine in Things so pretious.

Upwards thou dost weep.
Heavn's bosome drinks the gentle stream,
Where th'milky rivers creep,
Thine floates above; & is the cream.
Waters above th'Heavns, what they be
We'are taught best by thy TEARES & thee.

Every morn from hence
A brisk Cherub somthing sippes
Whose sacred influence
Addes sweetnes to his sweetest Lippes,
Then to his musick. And his song
Tasts of this Breakfast all day long.

Not in the evening's eyes
When they Red with weeping are
For the Sun that dyes,
Sitts sorrow with a face so fair,
No where but here did ever meet
Sweetnesse so sad, sadnesse so sweet.

When sorrow would be seen
In her brightest majesty
(For she is a Queen)
Then is she drest by none but thee.
Then, & only then, she weares
Her proudest pearles; I mean, thy Teares.

The deaw no more will weep
The primrose's pale cheek to deck,
The deaw no more will sleep
Nuzzel'd in the lilly's neck;
Much rather would it be thy Tear,
And leave them Both to tremble here.

There's no need at all
That the balsom-sweating bough
So coyly should let fall
His med'cinable teares; for now
Nature hath learn't to'extract a deaw
More soveraign & sweet from you.

Yet let the poore drops weep
(Weeping is the ease of woe)
Softly let them creep,
Sad that they are vanquish't so.
They, though to others no releife,
Balsom may be, for their own greife.

Such the maiden gemme
By the purpling vine put on,
Peeps from her parent stemme
And blushes at the bridegroomes sun.
This watry Blossom of thy eyn,
Ripe, will make the richer wine.

When some new bright Guest
Takes up among the starres a room,
And Heavn will make a feast,
Angels with crystall violls come
And draw from these full eyes of thine
Their master's Water: their own Wine.

Golden though he be,
Golden Tagus murmures tho;
Were his way by thee,
Content & quiet he would goe.
So much more rich would he esteem
Thy sylver, then his golden stream.

Well does the May that lyes
Smiling in thy cheeks, confesse
The April in thine eyes.
Mutuall sweetnesse they expresse.
No April ere lent kinder showres,
Nor May return'd more faithfull flowres.

O cheeks! Bedds of chast loves
By your own showres seasonably dash't.
Eyes! nests of milky doves
In your own wells decently washt.
O wit of love! that thus could place
Fountain & Garden in one face.

O sweet Contest; of woes
With loves, of teares with smiles disputing!
O fair, & Freindly Foes,
Each other kissing & confuting!
While rain & sunshine, Cheekes & Eyes
Close in kind contrarietyes.

But can these fair Flouds be
Freinds with the bosom fires that fill you!
Can so great flames agree
Æternall Teares should thus distill thee!
O flouds, o fires! o suns, ô showres!
Mixt & made freinds by love's sweet powres.

Twas his well-pointed dart
That digg'd these wells, & drest this wine;
And taught the wounded HEART
The way into these weeping Eyn.
Vain loves avant! bold hands forbear!
The lamb hath dipp't his white foot here.

And now where're he strayes,
Among the Galilean mountaines,
Or more unwellcome wayes,
He's followed by two faithfull fountaines;
Two walking baths; two weeping motions;
Portable, & compendious oceans.

O Thou, thy lord's fair store!
In thy so rich & rare expenses,
Even when he show'd most poor,
He might provoke the wealth of Princes.
What Prince's wanton'st pride e're could
Wash with Sylver, wipe with Gold?

Who is that King, but he
Who calls't his Crown to be call'd thine,
That thus can boast to be
Waited on by a wandring mine,
A voluntary mint, that strowes
Warm sylver shoures where're he goes!

O pretious Prodigall!
Fair spend-thrift of thy self! thy measure
(Mercilesse love!) is all.
Even to the last Pearle in thy threasure.
All places, Times, & objects be
Thy teare's sweet opportunity.

Does the day-starre rise?
Still thy starres doe fall & fall;
Does day close his eyes?
Still the Fountain weeps for all.
Let night or day doe what they will,
Thou hast thy task; thou weepest still.

Does thy song lull the air;
Thy falling teares keep faithfull time.
Does thy sweet-breath'd prayer
Up in clouds of incense climb?
Still at each sigh, that is, each stop,
A bead, that is, A Tear, does drop.

At these thy weeping gates,
(Watching their watry motion)
Each winged moment waits,
Takes his Tear, & gets him gone.
By thine Ey's tinct enobled thus
Time layes him up; he 's pretious.

Not, so long she lived,
Shall thy tomb report of thee;
But, so long she greived,
Thus must we date thy memory.
Others by moments, months, & yeares
Measure their ages; thou, by Teares.

So doe perfumes expire.
So sigh tormented sweets, opprest
With proud unpittying fires.
Such Teares the suffring Rose that 's vext
With ungentle flames does shed,
Sweating in a too warm bed.

Say, ye bright brothers,
The fugitive sons of those fair Eyes
Your fruitfull mothers !
What make you here ? what hopes can tice
You to be born ? what cause can borrow
You from those nests of noble sorrow ?

Whither away so fast ?
For sure the sordid earth
Your Sweetnes cannot tast
Nor does the dust deserve your birth.
Sweet, whither hast you then ? o say
Why you trip so fast away ?

We goe not to seek,
The darlings of Auroras bed,
The rose's modest Cheek
Nor the violet's humble head,
Though the Feild's eyes too WEEPERS be
Because they want such TEARES as we.

Much lesse mean we to trace
The Fortune of inferior gemmes,
Preferr'd to some proud face
Or pertch't upon fear'd Diadems.
Crown'd Heads are toyes. We goe to meet
A worthy object, our Lord's FEET.

Richard Crashaw.

Hymn to Saint Teresa.

LOve, thou art Absolute sole lord
Of Life & Death. To prove the word,
Wee'l now appeal to none of all
Those thy old Souldiers, Great & tall,
Ripe Men of Martyrdom, that could reach down
With strong armes, their triumphant crown;
Such as could with lusty breath
Speak lowd into the face of death
Their Great Lord's glorious name, to none
Of those whose spatious Bosomes spread a throne
For Love at larg to fill; spare blood & sweat,
And see him take a private seat,
Making his mansion in the mild
And milky soul of a soft child.
Scarse has she learn't to lisp the name
Of Martyr; yet she thinks it shame
Life should so long play with that breath
Which spent can buy so brave a death.
She never undertook to know
What death with love should have to doe;
Nor has she e're yet understood
Why to show love, she should shed blood,
Yet though she cannot tell you why,
She can Love, & she can Dy.
Scarse has she Blood enough to make
A guilty sword blush for her sake:
Yet has she'a Heart dares hope to prove
How much lesse strong is Death then Love.

Be love but there; let poor six yeares
Be pos'd with the maturest Feares
Man trembles at, you straight shall find
LOVE knowes no nonage, nor the MIND.
'Tis LOVE, not YEARES or LIMBS that can
Make the Martyr, or the man.
LOVE touch't her HEART, & lo it beates
High, & burnes with such brave heates;
Such thirsts to dy, as dares drink up,
A thousand cold deaths in one cup.
Good reason. For she breathes All fire.
Her weake brest heaves with strong desire
Of what she may with fruitles wishes
Seek for amongst her MOTHER'S Kisses.
Since 'tis not to be had at home
She'l travail to a Martyrdom.
No home for hers confesses she
But where she may a Martyr be.
She'l to the Moores; And trade with them,
For this unvalued Diadem.
She'l offer them her dearest Breath,
With CHRIST'S Name in't, in change for death.
She'l bargain with them; & will give
Them GOD; teach them how to live
In him: or, if they this deny,
For him she'l teach them how to DY.
So shall she leave amongst them sown
Her LORD'S Blood; or at lest her own.
FAREWEL then, all the world! Adieu.
TERESA is no more for you.
Farewell, all pleasures, sports, & joyes,
(Never till now esteemed toyes)
Farewell what ever deare may be,

MOTHER'S armes or FATHER'S knee.
Farewell house, & farewell home!
SHE'S for the Moores, & MARTYRDOM.
SWEET, not so fast! lo thy fair Spouse
Whom thou seekst with so swift vowes,
Calls thee back, & bidds thee come
T'embrace a milder MARTYRDOM.
Blest powres forbid, Thy tender life
Should bleed upon a barbarous knife;
Or some base hand have power to race
Thy Brest's chast cabinet, & uncase
A soul kept there so sweet, ô no;
Wise heavn will never have it so.
THOU art Love's victime; & must dy
A death more mysticall & high.
Into love's armes thou shalt let fall
A still-surviving funerall.
His is the DART must make the DEATH
Whose stroke shall tast thy hallow'd breath;
A Dart thrice dip't in that rich flame
Which writes thy spouse's radiant Name
Upon the roof of Heav'n; where ay
It shines, & with a soveraign ray
Beates bright upon the burning faces
Of soules which in that name's sweet graces
Find everlasting smiles. So rare,
So spirituall, pure, & fair
Must be th'immortall instrument
Upon whose choice point shall be sent
A life so lov'd; And that there be
Fitt executioners for Thee,
The fair'st & first-born sons of fire
Blest SERAPHIM, shall leave their quire

And turn love's souldiers, upon THEE
To exercise their archerie.
O how oft shalt thou complain
Of a sweet & subtle PAIN;
Of intolerable JOYES;
Of a DEATH, in which who dyes
Loves his death, and dyes again;
And would for ever so be slain.
And lives, & dyes; and knowes not why
To live, But that he thus may never leave to DY.
How kindly will thy gentle HEART
Kisse the sweetly-killing DART!
And close in his embraces keep
Those delicious Wounds, that weep
Balsom to heal themselves with. Thus
When These thy DEATHS, so numerous,
Shall all at last dy into one,
And melt thy Soul's sweet mansion;
Like a soft lump of incense, hasted
By too hott a fire, & wasted
Into perfuming clouds, so fast
Shalt thou exhale to Heavn at last
In a resolving SIGH, and then
O what? Ask not the Tongues of men.
Angells cannot tell, suffice,
Thy selfe shall feel thine own full joyes
And hold them fast for ever. There
So soon as thou shalt first appear,
The MOON of maidens starrs, thy white
MISTRESSE, attended by such bright
Soules as thy shining self, shall come
And in her first rankes make thee room;
Where 'mongst her snowy family

Immortall wellcomes wait for thee.
  O what delight, when reveal'd LIFE shall stand
And teach thy lipps heav'n with his hand;
On which thou now maist to thy wishes
Heap up thy consecrated kisses.
What joyes shall seize thy soul, when she
Bending her blessed eyes on thee
(Those second Smiles of Heav'n) shall dart
Her mild rayes through thy melting heart!
  Angels, thy old freinds, there shall greet thee
Glad at their own home now to meet thee.
  All thy good WORKES which went before
And waited for thee, at the door,
Shall own thee there; and all in one
Weave a constellation
Of CROWNS, with which the KING thy spouse
Shall build up thy triumphant browes.
  All thy old woes shall now smile on thee
And thy paines sitt bright upon thee.
All thy SUFFRINGS be divine.
TEARES shall take comfort, & turn gemms,
And WRONGS repent to Diademms.
Ev'n thy Deaths shall live; & new
Dresse the soul that erst they slew.
Thy wounds shall blush to such bright scarres
As keep account of the LAMB'S warres.
  Those rare WORKES where thou shalt leave writt
Love's noble history, with witt
Taught thee by none but him, while here
They feed our soules, shall cloth THINE there.
Each heavnly word by whose hid flame
Our hard Hearts shall strike fire, the same
Shall flourish on thy browes, & be

Both fire to us & flame to thee;
Whose light shall live bright in thy FACE
By glory, in our hearts by grace.
  Thou shalt look round about, & see
Thousands of crown'd Soules throng to be
Themselves thy crown; sons of thy vowes
The virgin-births with which thy soveraign spouse
Made fruitfull thy fair soul; Goe now
And with them all about thee bow
To Him. Put on (hee'l say) put on
(My rosy love) That thy rich zone
Sparkling with the sacred flames
Of thousand soules, whose happy names
Heav'n keeps upon thy score (Thy bright
Life brought them first to kisse the light
That kindled them to starrs,) and so
Thou with the LAMB, thy lord, shalt goe;
And whereso'ere he setts his white
Stepps, walk with HIM those wayes of light
Which who in death would live to see,
Must learn in life to dy like thee.

Richard Crashaw.

Regeneration.

A Ward, and still in bonds, one day
            I stole abroad,
It was high-spring, and all the way
      Primros'd, and hung with shade;
      Yet, was it frost within,
            And surly winds
Blasted my infant buds, and sinne
      Like Clouds ecclips'd my mind.

Storm'd thus; I straight perceiv'd my spring
Meere stage, and show,
My walke a monstrous, mountain'd thing
Rough-cast with Rocks, and snow;
And as a Pilgrims Eye
Far from reliefe,
Measures the melancholy skye
Then drops, and rains for griefe,

So sigh'd I upwards still, at last
'Twixt steps, and falls
I reach'd the pinacle, where plac'd
I found a paire of scales,
I tooke them up and layd
In th'one late paines,
The other smoake, and pleasures weigh'd
But prov'd the heavier graines;

With that, some cryed, *Away*; straight I
Obey'd, and led
Full East, a faire, fresh field could spy,
Some call'd it, *Jacobs Bed*;
A Virgin-soile, which no
Rude feet ere trod,
Where (since he stept there,) only go
Prophets, and friends of God.

Here, I repos'd; but scarse well set,
A grove descryed
Of stately height, whose branches met
And mixt on every side;
I entred, and once in
(Amaz'd to see't,)
Found all was chang'd, and a new spring
Did all my senses greet;

The unthrift Sunne shot vitall gold
A thousand peeces,
And heaven its azure did unfold
Checqur'd with snowie fleeces,
The aire was all in spice
And every bush
A garland wore; Thus fed my Eyes
But all the Eare lay hush.

Only a little Fountain lent
Some use for Eares,
And on the dumbe shades language spent
The Musick of her teares;
I drew her neere, and found
The Cisterne full
Of divers stones, some bright, and round,
Others ill-shap'd, and dull.

The first (pray marke,) as quick as light
Danc'd through the floud,
But, th'last more heavy then the night
Nail'd to the Center stood;
I wonder'd much, but tyr'd
At last with thought,
My restless Eye that still desir'd
As strange an object brought;

It was a banke of flowers, where I descried
(Though 'twas mid-day,)
Some fast asleepe, others broad-eyed
And taking in the Ray,
Here musing long, I heard
A rushing wind
Which still increas'd, but whence it stirr'd
No where I could not find;

I turn'd me round, and to each shade
Dispatch'd an Eye,
To see, if any leafe had made
Least motion, or Reply,
But while I listning sought
My mind to ease
By knowing, where 'twas, or where not,
It whisper'd; *Where I please.*

Lord, then said I, *On me one breath,*
And let me dye before my death!

Henry Vaughan.

The Retreate.

HAppy those early dayes! when I
Shin'd in my Angell-infancy.
Before I understood this place
Appointed for my second race,
Or taught my soul to fancy ought
But a white, Celestiall thought,
When yet I had not walkt above
A mile, or two, from my first love,
And looking back (at that short space,)
Could see a glimpse of his bright-face;
When on some *gilded Cloud,* or *flowre*
My gazing soul would dwell an houre,
And in those weaker glories spy
Some shadows of eternity;
Before I taught my tongue to wound
My Conscience with a sinfull sound,
Or had the black art to dispence
A sev'rall sinne to ev'ry sence,

But felt through all this fleshly dresse
Bright *shootes* of everlastingnesse.
O how I long to travell back
And tread again that ancient track!
That I might once more reach that plaine,
Where first I left my glorious traine,
From whence th' Inlightned spirit sees
That shady City of Palme trees;
But (ah!) my soul with too much stay
Is drunk, and staggers in the way.
Some men a forward motion love,
But I by backward steps would move,
And when this dust falls to the urn
In that state I came return.

Henry Vaughan.

ROM. CAP. 8. VER. 19.

Etenim res Creatæ exerto Capite observantes expectant revelationem Filiorum Dei.

AND do they so? have they a Sense
Of ought but Influence?
Can they their heads lift, and expect,
And grone too? why th'Elect
Can do no more: my volumes sed
They were all dull, and dead,
They judg'd them senslesse, and their state
Wholly Inanimate.
Go, go; Seal up thy looks,
And burn thy books.

I would I were a stone, or tree,
Or flowre by pedigree,
Or some poor high-way herb, or Spring
To flow, or bird to sing!
Then should I (tyed to one sure state,)
All day expect my date;
But I am sadly loose, and stray
A giddy blast each way;
O let me not thus range!
Thou canst not change.

Sometimes I sit with thee, and tarry
An hour, or so, then vary.
Thy other Creatures in this Scene
Thee only aym, and mean;
Some rise to seek thee, and with heads
Erect peep from their beds;
Others, whose birth is in the tomb.
And cannot quit the womb,
Sigh there, and grone for thee,
Their liberty.

O let not me do lesse! shall they
Watch, while I sleep, or play?
Shall I thy mercies still abuse
With fancies, friends, or newes?
O brook it not! thy bloud is mine,
And my soul should be thine;
O brook it not! why wilt thou stop
After whole showres one drop?
Sure, thou wilt joy to see
Thy sheep with thee.

Henry Vaughan.

Man.

WEighing the stedfastness and state
Of some mean things which here below reside,
Where birds like watchful Clocks the noiseless date
And Intercourse of times divide,
Where Bees at night get home and hive, and flowrs
Early, aswel as late,
Rise with the Sun, and set in the same bowrs;

I would (said I) my God would give
The staidness of these things to man! for these
To his divine appointments ever cleave,
And no new business breaks their peace;
The birds nor sow, nor reap, yet sup and dine,
The flowres without clothes live,
Yet *Solomon* was never drest so fine.

Man hath stil either toyes, or Care,
He hath no root, nor to one place is ty'd,
But ever restless and Irregular
About this Earth doth run and ride,
He knows he hath a home, but scarce knows where,
He sayes it is so far
That he hath quite forgot how to go there.

He knocks at all doors, strays and roams,
Nay hath not so much wit as some stones have
Which in the darkest nights point to their homes,
By some hid sense their Maker gave;
Man is the shuttle, to whose winding quest
And passage through these looms
God order'd motion, but ordain'd no rest.

Henry Vaughan.

Ascension-Hymn.

THey are all gone into the world of light!
And I alone sit lingring here;
Their very memory is fair and bright,
And my sad thoughts doth clear.

It glows and glitters in my cloudy brest
Like stars upon some gloomy grove,
Or those faint beams in which this hill is drest,
After the Sun's remove.

I see them walking in an Air of glory,
Whose light doth trample on my days:
My days, which are at best but dull and hoary,
Meer glimering and decays.

O holy hope! and high humility,
High as the Heavens above!
These are your walks, and you have shew'd them me
To kindle my cold love.

Dear, beauteous death! the Jewel of the Just,
Shining no where, but in the dark;
What mysteries do lie beyond thy dust;
Could man outlook that mark!

He that hath found some fledg'd birds nest, may know
At first sight, if the bird be flown;
But what fair Well, or Grove he sings in now,
That is to him unknown.

And yet, as Angels in some brighter dreams
　　Call to the soul, when man doth sleep:
So some strange thoughts transcend our wonted theams,
　　And into glory peep.

If a star were confin'd into a Tomb
　　Her captive flames must needs burn there;
But when the hand that lockt her up, gives room,
　　She'l shine through all the sphære.

O Father of eternal life, and all
　　Created glories under thee!
Resume thy spirit from this world of thrall
　　Into true liberty.

Either disperse these mists, which blot and fill
　　My perspective (still) as they pass,
Or else remove me hence unto that hill,
　　Where I shall need no glass.

Henry Vaughan.

AS time one day by me did pass
　Through a large dusky glasse
　He held, I chanc'd to look
　And spyed his curious book
Of past days, where sad Heav'n did shed
A mourning light upon the dead.

Many disordered lives I saw
　And foul records which thaw
　My kinde eyes still, but in
　A fair, white page of thin
And ev'n, smooth lines, like the Suns rays,
Thy name was writ, and all thy days.

O bright and happy Kalendar!
    Where youth shines like a star
    All pearl'd with tears, and may
    Teach age, *The Holy way*;
Where through thick pangs, high agonies
Faith into life breaks, and death dies.

As some meek *night-piece* which day quails,
    To candle-light unveils:
    So by one beamy line
    From thy bright lamp did shine,
In the same page thy humble grave
Set with green herbs, glad hopes and brave.

Here slept my thoughts dear mark! which dust
    Seem'd to devour, like rust;
    But dust (I did observe)
    By hiding doth preserve,
As we for long and sure recruits,
Candy with sugar our choice fruits.

O calm and sacred bed where lies
    In deaths dark mysteries
    A beauty far more bright
    Then the noons cloudless light
For whose dry dust green branches bud
And robes are bleach'd in the *Lambs* blood.

Sleep happy ashes! (blessed sleep!)
    While haplesse I still weep;
    Weep that I have out-liv'd
    My life, and unreliev'd
Must (soul-lesse shadow!) so live on,
Though life be dead, and my joys gone.

Henry Vaughan.

The dwelling-place

S. John, chap. 1. *ver.* 38, 39.

WHat happy, secret fountain,
Fair shade, or mountain,
Whose undiscover'd virgin glory
Boasts it this day, though not in story,
Was then thy dwelling? did some cloud
Fix'd to a Tent, descend and shrowd
My distrest Lord? or did a star
Becken'd by thee, though high and far,
In sparkling smiles haste gladly down
To lodge light, and increase her own?
My dear, dear God! I do not know
What lodged thee then, nor where, nor how;
But I am sure, thou dost now come
Oft to a narrow, homely room,
Where thou too hast but the least part,
My God, I mean *my sinful heart.*

Henry Vaughan.

The Night.

John 2. 3.

THrough that pure *Virgin-shrine,*
That sacred vail drawn o'r thy glorious noon
That men might look and live as Glo-worms shine,
And face the Moon:
Wise *Nicodemus* saw such light
As made him know his God by night.

Most blest believer he!
Who in that land of darkness and blinde eyes
Thy long expected healing wings could see,
When thou didst rise,
And what can never more be done,
Did at mid-night speak with the Sun!

O who will tell me, where
He found thee at that dead and silent hour!
What hallow'd solitary ground did bear
So rare a flower,
Within whose sacred leafs did lie
The fulness of the Deity.

No mercy-seat of gold,
No dead and dusty *Cherub*, nor carv'd stone,
But his own living works did my Lord hold
And lodge alone;
Where *trees* and *herbs* did watch and peep
And wonder, while the *Jews* did sleep.

Dear night! this worlds defeat;
The stop to busie fools; cares check and curb;
The day of Spirits; my souls calm retreat
Which none disturb!
Christs progress, and his prayer time;
The hours to which high Heaven doth chime.

Gods silent, searching flight:
When my Lords head is fill'd with dew, and all
His locks are wet with the clear drops of night;
His still, soft call;
His knocking time; The souls dumb watch,
When Spirits their fair kinred catch.

Were all my loud, evil days
Calm and unhaunted as is thy dark Tent,
Whose peace but by some *Angels* wing or voice
Is seldom rent;
Then I in Heaven all the long year
Would keep, and never wander here.

But living where the Sun
Doth all things wake, and where all mix and tyre
Themselves and others, I consent and run
To ev'ry myre,
And by this worlds ill-guiding light,
Erre more then I can do by night.

There is in God (some say)
A deep, but dazzling darkness; As men here
Say it is late and dusky, because they
See not all clear;
O for that night! where I in him
Might live invisible and dim.

Henry Vaughan.

The Water-fall.

With what deep murmurs through times silent stealth
Doth thy transparent, cool and watry wealth
Here flowing fall,
And chide, and call,
As if his liquid, loose Retinue staid
Lingring, and were of this steep place afraid,
The common pass
Where, clear as glass,

All must descend
Not to an end :
But quickned by this deep and rocky grave,
Rise to a longer course more bright and brave.

Dear stream ! dear bank, where often I
Have sate, and pleas'd my pensive eye,
Why, since each drop of thy quick store
Runs thither, whence it flow'd before,
Should poor souls fear a shade or night,
Who came (sure) from a sea of light ?
Or since those drops are all sent back
So sure to thee, that none doth lack,
Why should frail flesh doubt any more
That what God takes, hee'l not restore ?

O useful Element and clear !
My sacred wash and cleanser here,
My first consigner unto those
Fountains of life, where the Lamb goes ?
What sublime truths, and wholesome themes,
Lodge in thy mystical, deep streams !
Such as dull man can never finde
Unless that Spirit lead his minde,
Which first upon thy face did move,
And hatch'd all with his quickning love.
As this loud brooks incessant fall
In streaming rings restagnates all,
Which reach by course the bank, and then
Are no more seen, just so pass men.
O my invisible estate,
My glorious liberty, still late !
Thou art the Channel my soul seeks,
Not this with Cataracts and Creeks.

Henry Vaughan.

Quickness.

FAlse life! a foil and no more, when
Wilt thou be gone?
Thou foul deception of all men
That would not have the true come on.

Thou art a Moon-like toil; a blinde
Self-posing state;
A dark contest of waves and winde;
A meer tempestuous debate.

Life is a fix'd, discerning light,
A knowing Joy;
No chance, or fit: but ever bright,
And calm and full, yet doth not cloy.

'Tis such a blissful thing, that still
Doth vivifie,
And shine and smile, and hath the skill
To please without Eternity.

Thou art a toylsom Mole, or less,
A moving mist;
But life is, what none can express,
A quickness, which my God hath kist.

Henry Vaughan.

A Pastorall Hymne.

HAppy Choristers of Aire,
Who by your nimble flight draw neare
His throne, whose wondrous story
And unconfined glory
Your notes still Caroll, whom your sound
And whom your plumy pipes rebound.

Yet do the lazy Snailes no lesse
The greatnesse of our Lord confesse,
And those whom weight hath chain'd
And to the Earth restrain'd,
Their ruder voices do as well,
Yea and the speechlesse Fishes tell.

Great Lord, from whom each Tree receaves,
Then paies againe as rent, his leaves;
Thou dost in purple set
The Rose and Violet,
And giv'st the sickly Lilly white,
Yet in them all, thy name dost write.

John Hall.

And she washed his Feet with her Teares, and wiped them with the Hairs of her Head.

THe proud *Ægyptian* Queen, her *Roman* Guest,
(T'express her Love in Hight of State, and Pleasure)
With Pearl dissolv'd in Gold, did feast,
Both Food, and Treasure.

And now (dear Lord!) thy Lover, on the fair
And silver Tables of thy Feet, behold!
Pearl in her Tears, and in her Hair,
Offers thee Gold.

Edward Sherburne.

The Christians reply to the Phylosopher.

THe Good in Graves as Heavenly Seed are sown;
 And at the Saints first Spring, the General Doome,
Will rise, not by degrees, but fully blowne;
 When all the Angells to their Harvest come.

Cannot Almighty Heaven (since Flowers which pass
 Thaw'd through a Still, and there melt mingled too,
Are rais'd distinct in a poore Chymists Glass)
 Doe more in Graves then Men in Lymbecks doe?

God bred the Arts to make us more believe
 (By seeking Natures cover'd Misteries)
His darker Workes, that Faith may thence conceive
 He can do more then what our Reason sees.

O Coward Faith! Religion's trembling Guide!
 Whom even the dim-ey'd Arts must lead to see
What Nature only from our sloath does hide,
 Causes remote, which Faith's dark dangers be.

Religion, e're impos'd, should first be taught;
 Not seeme to dull obedience ready lay'd,
Then swallow'd strait for ease, but long be sought;
 And be by Reason councell'd, though not sway'd.

God has enough to humane kinde disclos'd;
 Our fleshly Garments he a while receiv'd,
And walk'd as if the Godhead were depos'd,
 Yet could be then but by a few believ'd.

The Faithless *Jews* will this at Doome confess,
 Who did suspect him for his low disguise:
But, if he could have made his vertue less,
 He had been more familiar to their Eyes.

Fraile Life! in which, through Mists of humane breath,
We grope for Truth, and make our Progress slow;
Because, by passion blinded, till by death,
Our Passions ending, we begin to know.

O rev'rend Death! whose looks can soon advise
Even scornfull Youth; whilst Priests their Doctrine wast,
Yet mocks us too; for he does make us wise,
When by his coming our Affaires are past.

O harmless Death! whom still the valiant brave,
The Wise expect, the Sorrowfull invite,
And all the Good embrace, who know the *Grave*,
A short dark passage to Eternal Light.

Sir William Davenant.

A Dialogue between The Resolved Soul and Created Pleasure.

COurage my Soul, now learn to wield
The weight of thine immortal Shield.
Close on thy Head thy Helmet bright.
Ballance thy Sword against the Fight.
See where an Army, strong as fair,
With silken Banners spreads the air.
Now, if thou bee'st that thing Divine,
In this day's Combat let it shine:
And shew that Nature wants an Art
To conquer one resolved Heart.

Pleasure. Welcome the Creations Guest,
Lord of Earth, and Heavens Heir.
Lay aside that Warlike Crest,
And of Nature's banquet share:
Where the Souls of fruits and flow'rs
Stand prepar'd to heighten yours.

Soul. I sup above, and cannot stay
To bait so long upon the way.

Pleasure. On these downy Pillows lye,
Whose soft Plumes will thither fly:
On these Roses strow'd so plain
Lest one Leaf thy Side should strain.

Soul. My gentler Rest is on a Thought,
Conscious of doing what I ought.

Pleasure. If thou bee'st with Perfumes pleas'd,
Such as oft the Gods appeas'd,
Thou in fragrant Clouds shalt show
Like another God below.

Soul. A Soul that knowes not to presume
Is Heaven's and its own perfume.

Pleasure. Every thing does seem to vie
Which should first attract thine Eye:
But since none deserves that grace,
In this Crystal view *thy* face.

Soul. When the Creator's skill is priz'd,
The rest is all but Earth disguis'd.

Pleasure. Heark how Musick then prepares
For thy Stay these charming Aires;
Which the posting Winds recall,
And suspend the Rivers Fall.

Soul. Had I but any time to lose,
On this I would it all dispose.
Cease Tempter. None can chain a mind
Whom this sweet Chordage cannot bind.

Chorus. *Earth cannot shew so brave a Sight*
As when a single Soul does fence
The Batteries of alluring Sense,
And Heaven views it with delight.
Then persevere: for still new Charges sound:
And if thou overcom'st thou shalt be crown'd.

Pleasure. All this fair, and cost, and sweet,
Which scatteringly doth shine,
Shall within one Beauty meet,
And she be only thine.

Soul. If things of Sight such Heavens be,
What Heavens are those we cannot see?

Pleasure. Where so e're thy Foot shall go
The minted Gold shall lie;
Till thou purchase all below,
And want new Worlds to buy.

Soul. Wer't not a price who'ld value Gold?
And that's worth nought that can be sold.

Pleasure. Wilt thou all the Glory have
That War or Peace commend?
Half the World shall be thy Slave
The other half thy Friend.

Soul. What Friends, if to my self untrue?
What Slaves, unless I captive you?

Pleasure. Thou shalt know each hidden Cause;
And see the future Time:
Try what depth the Centre draws;
And then to Heaven climb.

Soul. None thither mounts by the degree
Of Knowledge, but Humility.

Chorus. *Triumph, triumph, victorious Soul;*
The World has not one Pleasure more:
The rest does lie beyond the Pole,
And is thine everlasting Store.

Andrew Marvell.

The Coronet.

WHen for the Thorns with which I long, too long,
With many a piercing wound,
My Saviours head have crown'd,
I seek with Garlands to redress that Wrong:
Through every Garden, every Mead,
I gather flow'rs (my fruits are only flow'rs)
Dismantling all the fragrant Towers
That once adorn'd my Shepherdesses head.
And now when I have summ'd up all my store,
Thinking (so I my self deceive)
So rich a Chaplet thence to weave
As never yet the king of Glory wore:
Alas I find the Serpent old
That, twining in his speckled breast,
About the flow'rs disguis'd does fold,
With wreaths of Fame and Interest.

Ah, foolish Man, that would'st debase with them,
And mortal Glory, Heavens Diadem!
But thou who only could'st the Serpent tame
Either his slipp'ry knots at once untie,
And disintangle all his winding Snare:
Or shatter too with him my curious frame:
And let these wither, so that he may die,
Though set with Skill and chosen out with Care.
That they, while Thou on both their Spoils dost tread,
May crown thy Feet, that could not crown thy Head.

Andrew Marvell.

A Dialogue between the Soul and Body.

Soul. O Who shall, from this Dungeon, raise
A Soul inslav'd so many wayes?
With bolts of Bones, that fetter'd stands
In Feet; and manacled in Hands.
Here blinded with an Eye; and there
Deaf with the drumming of an Ear.
A Soul hung up, as 'twere, in Chains
Of Nerves, and Arteries, and Veins.
Tortur'd, besides each other part,
In a vain Head, and double Heart.

Body. O who shall me deliver whole,
From bonds of this Tyrannic Soul?
Which, stretcht upright, impales me so,
That mine own Precipice I go;
And warms and moves this needless Frame:
(A Fever could but do the same.)

And, wanting where its spight to try,
Has made me live to let me dye.
A Body that could never rest,
Since this ill Spirit it possest.

Soul. What Magick could me thus confine
Within anothers Grief to pine?
Where whatsoever it complain,
I feel, that cannot feel, the pain.
And all my Care its self employes,
That to preserve, which me destroys:
Constrain'd not only to indure
Diseases, but, whats worse, the Cure:
And ready oft the Port to gain,
Am Shipwrackt into Health again.

Body. But Physick yet could never reach
The Maladies Thou me dost teach;
Whom first the Cramp of Hope does Tear:
And then the Palsie Shakes of Fear.
The Pestilence of Love does heat:
Or Hatred's hidden Ulcer eat.
Joy's chearful Madness does perplex:
Or Sorrow's other Madness vex.
Which Knowledge forces me to know;
And Memory will not foregoe.
What but a Soul could have the wit
To build me up for Sin so fit?
So Architects do square and hew
Green Trees that in the Forest grew.

Andrew Marvell.

MISCELLANIES.

Elegies, Epistles, Satires, and Meditations.

Elegie.

His Picture.

HEre take my Picture; though I bid farewell,
Thine, in my heart, where my soule dwels, shall dwell.
'Tis like me now, but I dead, 'twill be more
When wee are shadowes both, then'twas before.
When weather-beaten I come backe; my hand,
Perhaps with rude oares torne, or Sun beams tann'd,
My face and brest of hairecloth, and my head
With cares rash sodaine stormes, being o'rspread,
My body'a sack of bones, broken within,
And powders blew staines scatter'd on my skinne;
If rivall fooles taxe thee to'have lov'd a man,
So foule, and course, as, Oh, I may seeme than,
This shall say what I was: and thou shalt say,
Doe his hurts reach mee? doth my worth decay?
Or doe they reach his judging minde, that hee
Should now love lesse, what hee did love to see?
That which in him was faire and delicate,
Was but the milke, which in loves childish state
Did nurse it: who now is growne strong enough
To feed on that, which to disused tasts seemes tough.

John Donne.

Elegie.

On his Mistris.

BY our first strange and fatall interview,
By all desires which thereof did ensue,
By our long starving hopes, by that remorse
Which my words masculine perswasive force
Begot in thee, and by the memory
Of hurts, which spies and rivals threatned me,
I calmly beg: But by thy fathers wrath,
By all paines, which want and divorcement hath,
I conjure thee, and all the oathes which I
And thou have sworne to seale joynt constancy,
Here I unsweare, and overswear them thus,
Thou shalt not love by wayes so dangerous.
Temper, ô faire Love, loves impetuous rage,
Be my true Mistris still, not my faign'd Page;
I'll goe, and, by thy kinde leave, leave behinde
Thee, onely worthy to nurse in my minde
Thirst to come backe; ô if thou die before,
My soule from other lands to thee shall soare.
Thy (else Almighty) beautie cannot move
Rage from the Seas, nor thy love teach them love,
Nor tame wilde Boreas harshnesse; Thou hast reade
How roughly hee in peeces shivered
Faire Orithea, whom he swore he lov'd.
Fall ill or good, 'tis madnesse to have prov'd
Dangers unurg'd; Feed on this flattery,
That absent Lovers one in th'other be.
Dissemble nothing, not a boy, nor change
Thy bodies habite, nor mindes; bee not strange

To thy selfe onely; All will spie in thy face
A blushing womanly discovering grace;
Richly cloath'd Apes, are call'd Apes, and as soone
Ecclips'd as bright we call the Moone the Moone.
Men of France, changeable Camelions,
Spittles of diseases, shops of fashions,
Loves fuellers, and the rightest company
Of Players, which upon the worlds stage be,
Will quickly know thee, and no lesse, alas!
Th'indifferent Italian, as we passe
His warme land, well content to thinke thee Page,
Will hunt thee with such lust, and hideous rage,
As *Lots* faire guests were vext. But none of these
Nor spungy hydroptique Dutch shall thee displease,
If thou stay here. O stay here, for, for thee
England is onely a worthy Gallerie,
To walke in expectation, till from thence
Our greatest King call thee to his presence.
When I am gone, dreame me some happinesse,
Nor let thy lookes our long hid love confesse,
Nor praise, nor dispraise me, nor blesse nor curse
Openly loves force, nor in bed fright thy Nurse
With midnights startings, crying out, oh, oh
Nurse, ô my love is slaine, I saw him goe
O'r the white Alpes alone; I saw him I,
Assail'd, fight, taken, stabb'd, bleed, fall, and die
Augure me better chance, except dread *Iove*
Thinke it enough for me to'have had thy love.

John Donne.

Satyre.

Kinde pitty chokes my spleene; brave scorn forbids
Those tears to issue which swell my eye-lids;
I must not laugh, nor weepe sinnes, and be wise,
Can railing then cure these worne maladies?
Is not our Mistresse faire Religion,
As worthy of all our Soules devotion,
As vertue was to the first blinded age?
Are not heavens joyes as valiant to asswage
Lusts, as earths honour was to them? Alas,
As wee do them in meanes, shall they surpasse
Us in the end, and shall thy fathers spirit
Meete blinde Philosophers in heaven, whose merit
Of strict life may be imputed faith, and heare
Thee, whom hee taught so easie wayes and neare
To follow, damn'd? O if thou dar'st, feare this;
This feare great courage, and high valour is.
Dar'st thou ayd mutinous Dutch, and dar'st thou lay
Thee in ships woodden Sepulchers, a prey
To leaders rage, to stormes, to shot, to dearth?
Dar'st thou dive seas, and dungeons of the earth?
Hast thou couragious fire to thaw the ice
Of frozen North discoueries? and thrise
Colder then Salamanders, like divine
Children in th'oven, fires of Spaine, and the line,
Whose countries limbecks to our bodies bee,
Canst thou for gaine beare? and must every hee
Which cryes not, Goddesse, to thy Mistresse, draw,
Or eate thy poysonous words? courage of straw!
O desperate coward, wilt thou seeme bold, and
To thy foes and his (who made thee to stand

Sentinell in his worlds garrison) thus yeeld,
And for forbidden warres, leave th'appointed field?
Know thy foes: The foule Devill (whom thou
Strivest to please,) for hate, not love, would allow
Thee faine, his whole Realme to be quit; and as
The worlds all parts wither away and passe,
So the worlds selfe, thy other lov'd foe, is
In her decrepit wayne, and thou loving this,
Dost love a withered and worne strumpet; last,
Flesh (it selfes death) and joyes which flesh can taste,
Thou lovest; and thy faire goodly soule, which doth
Give this flesh power to taste joy, thou dost loath.
Seeke true religion. O where? Mirreus
Thinking her unhous'd here, and fled from us,
Seekes her at Rome; there, because hee doth know
That shee was there a thousand yeares agoe,
He loves her ragges so, as wee here obey
The statecloth where the Prince sate yesterday.
Crantz to such brave Loves will not be inthrall'd,
But loves her onely, who at Geneva is call'd
Religion, plaine, simple, sullen, yong,
Contemptuous, yet unhansome; As among
Lecherous humors, there is one that judges
No wenches wholsome, but course country drudges,
Graius stayes still at home here, and because
Some Preachers, vile ambitious bauds, and lawes
Still new like fashions, bid him thinke that shee
Which dwels with us, is onely perfect, hee
Imbraceth her, whom his Godfathers will
Tender to him, being tender, as Wards still
Take such wives as their Guardians offer, or
Pay valewes. Carelesse Phrygius doth abhorre
All, because all cannot be good, as one

Knowing some women whores, dares marry none.
Graccus loves all as one, and thinkes that so
As women do in divers countries goe
In divers habits, yet are still one kinde,
So doth, so is Religion; and this blind-
nesse too much light breeds; but unmoved thou
Of force must one, and forc'd but one allow;
And the right; aske thy father which is shee,
Let him aske his; though truth and falshood bee
Neare twins, yet truth a little elder is;
Be busie to seeke her, beleeve mee this,
Hee 's not of none, nor worst, that seekes the best.
To adore, or scorne an image, or protest,
May all be bad; doubt wisely; in strange way
To stand inquiring right, is not to stray;
To sleepe, or runne wrong, is. On a huge hill,
Cragged, and steep, Truth stands, and hee that will
Reach her, about must, and about must goe;
And what the hills suddennes resists, winne so;
Yet strive so, that before age, deaths twilight,
Thy Soule rest, for none can worke in that night.
To will, implyes delay, therefore now doe:
Hard deeds, the bodies paines; hard knowledge too
The mindes indeavours reach, and mysteries
Are like the Sunne, dazling, yet plaine to all eyes.
Keepe the truth which thou hast found; men do not stand
In so ill case here, that God hath with his hand
Sign'd Kings blanck-charters to kill whom they hate,
Nor are they Vicars, but hangmen to Fate.
Foole and wretch, wilt thou let thy Soule be tyed
To mans lawes, by which she shall not be tryed
At the last day? Oh, will it then boot thee
To say a Philip, or a Gregory,

A Harry, or a Martin taught thee this?
Is not this excuse for mere contraries,
Equally strong? cannot both sides say so?
That thou mayest rightly obey power, her bounds know;
Those past, her nature, and name is chang'd; to be
Then humble to her is idolatrie.
As streames are, Power is; those blest flowers that dwell
At the rough streames calme head, thrive and do well,
But having left their roots, and themselves given
To the streames tyrannous rage, alas, are driven
Through mills, and rockes, and woods, and at last, almost
Consum'd in going, in the sea are lost:
So perish Soules, which more chuse mens unjust
Power from God claym'd, then God himselfe to trust.

John Donne.

To Sir H. W. *at his going Ambassador to Venice.*

AFter those reverend papers, whose soule is
  Our good and great Kings lov'd hand and fear'd name,
By which to you he derives much of his,
  And (how he may) makes you almost the same,

A Taper of his Torch, a copie writ
  From his Originall, and a faire beame
Of the same warme, and dazeling Sun, though it
  Must in another Sphere his vertue streame:

After those learned papers which your hand
  Hath stor'd with notes of use and pleasure too,
From which rich treasury you may command
  Fit matter whether you will write or doe:

After those loving papers, where friends send
With glad griefe, to your Sea-ward steps, farewel,
Which thicken on you now, as prayers ascend
To heaven in troupes at'a good mans passing bell:

Admit this honest paper, and allow
It such an audience as your selfe would aske;
What you must say at Venice this meanes now,
And hath for nature, what you have for taske:

To sweare much love, not to be chang'd before
Honour alone will to your fortune fit;
Nor shall I then honour your fortune, more
Then I have done your honour wanting it.

But'tis an easier load (though both oppresse)
To want, then governe greatnesse, for wee are
In that, our owne and onely businesse,
In this, wee must for others vices care;

'Tis therefore well your spirits now are plac'd
In their last Furnace, in activity;
Which fits them (Schooles and Courts and Warres o'rpast)
To touch and test in any best degree.

For mee, (if there be such a thing as I)
Fortune (if there be such a thing as shee)
Spies that I beare so well her tyranny,
That she thinks nothing else so fit for mee;

But though she part us, to heare my oft prayers
For your increase, God is as neere mee here;
And to send you what I shall begge, his staires
In length and ease are alike every where.

John Donne.

To the Countesse of Bedford.

HOnour is so sublime perfection,
And so refinde; that when God was alone
And creaturelesse at first, himselfe had none;

But as of the elements, these which wee tread,
Produce all things with which wee'are joy'd or fed,
And, those are barren both above our head:

So from low persons doth all honour flow;
Kings, whom they would have honoured, to us show,
And but *direct* our honour, not *bestow*.

For when from herbs the pure part must be wonne
From grosse, by Stilling, this is better done
By despis'd dung, then by the fire or Sunne.

Care not then, Madame,'how low your praysers lye;
In labourers balads oft more piety
God findes, then in *Te Deums* melodie.

And, ordinance rais'd on Towers, so many mile
Send not their voice, nor last so long a while
As fires from th'earths low vaults in *Sicil* Isle.

Should I say I liv'd darker then were true,
Your radiation can all clouds subdue;
But one, 'tis best light to contemplate you.

You, for whose body God made better clay,
Or tooke Soules stuffe such as shall late decay,
Or such as needs small change at the last day.

This, as an Amber drop enwraps a Bee,
Covering discovers your quicke Soule; that we
May in your through-shine front your hearts thoughts see.

You teach (though wee learne not) a thing unknowne
To our late times, the use of specular stone,
Through which all things within without were shown.

Of such were Temples; so and of such you are;
Beeing and *seeming* is your equall care,
And *vertues* whole *summe* is but *know* and *dare*.

But as our Soules of growth and Soules of sense
Have birthright of our reasons Soule, yet hence
They fly not from that, nor seeke presidence:

Natures first lesson, so, discretion,
Must not grudge zeale a place, nor yet keepe none,
Not banish it selfe, nor religion.

Discretion is a wisemans Soule, and so
Religion is a Christians, and you know
How these are one; her *yea*, is not her *no*.

Nor may we hope to sodder still and knit
These two, and dare to breake them; nor must wit
Be colleague to religion, but be it.

In those poor types of God (round circles) so
Religions tipes the peeclesse centers flow,
And are in all the lines which all wayes goe.

If either ever wrought in you alone
Or principally, then religion
Wrought your ends, and your wayes discretion.

Goe thither stil, goe the same way you went,
Who so would change, do covet or repent;
Neither can reach you, great and innocent.

John Donne.

<Valediction to Life.>

FArewel ye guilded follies, pleasing troubles,
Farewel ye honour'd rags, ye glorious bubbles;
Fame's but a hollow echo, gold pure clay,
Honour the darling but of one short day.
Beauty (th'eyes idol) but a damasked skin,
State but a golden prison, to keepe in
And torture free-born minds; imbroidered trains
Meerly but Pageants, proudly swelling vains,
And blood ally'd to greatness, is a loane
Inherited, not purchased, not our own.
Fame, honor, beauty, state, train, blood and birth,
Are but the fading blossomes of the earth.

I would be great, but that the Sun doth still
Level his rayes against the rising hill:
I would be high, but see the proudest Oak
Most subject to the rending Thunder-stroke;
I would be rich, but see men too unkind
Dig in the bowels of the richest mine;
I would be wise, but that I often see
The Fox suspected whilst the Ass goes free;
I would be fair, but see the fair and proud
Like the bright sun, oft setting in a cloud;
I would be poor, but know the humble grass
Still trampled on by each unworthy Asse:
Rich, hated; wise, suspected; scorn'd, if poor;
Great, fear'd; fair, tempted; hight, stil envied more:
I have wish'd all, but now I wish for neither,
Great, high, rich, wise, nor fair, poor I'l be rather.

Would the world now adopt me for her heir,
Would beauties Queen entitle me the Fair,
Fame speak me fortune's Minion, could I vie
Angels with India, with a speaking eye
Command bare heads, bow'd knees, strike Justice dumb
As wel as blind and lame, or give a tongue
To stones, by Epitaphs, be called great Master
In the loose rhimes of every Poetaster;
Could I be more then any man that lives,
Great, fair, rich, wise all in Superlatives;
Yet I more freely would these gifts resign
Then ever fortune would have made them mine,
And hold one minute of this holy leasure,
Beyond the riches of this empty pleasure.

Welcom pure thoughts, welcom ye silent groves,
These guests, these Courts, my soul most dearly loves,
Now the wing'd people of the Skie shall sing
My cheerful Anthems to the gladsome Spring;
A Pray'r book now shall be my looking-glasse,
Wherein I will adore sweet vertues face.
Here dwell no hateful looks, no Pallace cares,
No broken vows dwell here, nor pale-faced fears,
Then here I'l sit and sigh my hot loves folly,
And learn t'affect an holy melancholy.
And if contentment be a stranger, then
I'l nere look for it, but in heaven again.

Ignoto.

An Elegie upon the death of the Deane of Pauls, *D*r. Iohn Donne.

CAn we not force from widdowed Poetry,
Now thou art dead (Great DONNE) one Elegie
To crowne thy Hearse? Why yet dare we not trust
Though with unkneaded dowe-bak't prose thy dust,
Such as the uncisor'd Churchman from the flower
Of fading Rhetorique, short liv'd as his houre,
Dry as the sand that measures it, should lay
Upon thy Ashes, on the funerall day?
Have we no voice, no tune? Did'st thou dispense
Through all our language, both the words and sense?
'Tis a sad truth; The Pulpit may her plaine,
And sober Christian precepts still retaine,
Doctrines it may, and wholesome Uses frame,
Grave Homilies, and Lectures, But the flame
Of thy brave Soule, that shot such heat and light,
As burnt our earth, and made our darknesse bright,
Committed holy Rapes upon our Will,
Did through the eye the melting heart distill;
And the deepe knowledge of darke truths so teach,
As sense might judge, what phansie could not reach;
Must be desir'd for ever. So the fire,
That fills with spirit and heat the Delphique quire,
Which kindled first by thy Promethean breath,
Glow'd here a while, lies quench't now in thy death;
The Muses garden with Pedantique weedes
O'rspred, was purg'd by thee; The lazie seeds

Of servile imitation throwne away;
And fresh invention planted, Thou didst pay
The debts of our penurious bankrupt age;
Licentious thefts, that make poëtique rage
A Mimique fury, when our soules must bee
Possest, or with Anacreons Extasie,
Or Pindars, not their owne; The subtle cheat
Of slie Exchanges, and the jugling feat
Of two-edg'd words, or whatsoever wrong
By ours was done the Greeke, or Latine tongue,
Thou hast redeem'd, and open'd Us a Mine
Of rich and pregnant phansie, drawne a line
Of masculine expression, which had good
Old Orpheus seene, Or all the ancient Brood
Our superstitious fooles admire, and hold
Their lead more precious, then thy burnish't Gold,
Thou hadst beene their Exchequer, and no more
They each in others dust had rak'd for Ore.
Thou shalt yield no precedence, but of time,
And the blinde fate of language, whose tun'd chime
More charmes the outward sense; Yet thou maist claime
From so great disadvantage greater fame,
Since to the awe of thy imperious wit
Our stubborne language bends, made only fit
With her tough-thick-rib'd hoopes to gird about
Thy Giant phansie, which had prov'd too stout
For their soft melting Phrases. As in time
They had the start, so did they cull the prime
Buds of invention many a hundred yeare,
And left the rifled fields, besides the feare
To touch their Harvest, yet from those bare lands
Of what is purely thine, thy only hands
(And that thy smallest worke) have gleaned more

Then all those times, and tongues could reape before;
But thou art gone, and thy strict lawes will be
Too hard for Libertines in Poetrie.
They will repeale the goodly exil'd traine
Of gods and goddesses, which in thy just raigne
Were banish'd nobler Poems, now, with these
The silenc'd tales o'th'Metamorphoses
Shall stuffe their lines, and swell the windy Page,
Till Verse refin'd by thee, in this last Age
Turne ballad rime, Or those old Idolls bee
Ador'd againe, with new apostasie;
Oh, pardon mee, that breake with untun'd verse
The reverend silence that attends thy herse,
Whose awfull solemne murmures were to thee
More then these faint lines, A loud Elegie,
That did proclaime in a dumbe eloquence
The death of all the Arts, whose influence
Growne feeble, in these panting numbers lies
Gasping short winded Accents, and so dies:
So doth the swiftly turning wheele not stand
In th'instant we withdraw the moving hand,
But some small time maintaine a faint weake course
By vertue of the first impulsive force:
And so whil'st I cast on thy funerall pile
Thy crowne of Bayes, Oh, let it crack a while,
And spit disdaine, till the devouring flashes
Suck all the moysture up, then turne to ashes.
I will not draw the(e) envy to engrosse
All thy perfections. or weepe all our losse;
Those are too numerous for an Elegie,
And this too great, to be express'd by mee.
Though every pen should share a distinct part,
Yet art thou Theme enough to tyre all Art;

Let others carve the rest, it shall suffice
I on thy Tombe this Epitaph incise.

Here lies a King, that rul'd as hee thought fit
The universall Monarchy of wit;
Here lie two Flamens, and both those the best,
Apollo's first, at last, the true Gods Priest.

Thomas Carew.

To my worthy friend Mr. George Sandys.

I Presse not to the Quire, nor dare I greet
The holy Place with my unhallow'd feet:
My unwasht Muse pollutes not things Divine,
Nor mingles her prophaner notes with thine;
Here, humbly at the Porch, she listning stayes,
And with glad eares sucks in thy Sacred Layes.
So, devout Penitents of old were wont,
Some without doore, and some beneath the Font,
To stand and heare the Churches Liturgies,
Yet not assist the solemne Exercise.
Sufficeth her, that she a Lay-place gaine,
To trim thy Vestments, or but beare thy traine:
Though nor in Tune, nor Wing, She reach thy Larke,
Her Lyricke feet may dance before the Arke.
Who knowes, but that Her wandring eyes, that run
Now hunting Glow-wormes, may adore the Sun.
A pure Flame may, shot by Almighty Power
Into my brest, the earthy flame devoure:
My Eyes, in Penitentiall dew may steepe

That bryne, which they for sensuall love did weepe:
So (though 'gainst Natures course) fire may be quencht
With fire, and water be with water drencht.
Perhaps, my restlesse Soule, tyr'd with pursuit
Of mortall beautie, seeking without fruit
Contentment there; which hath not, when enjoy'd,
Quencht all her thirst, nor satisfi'd, though cloy'd;
Weary of her vaine search below, above
In the first Faire may find th' immortall Love.
Prompted by thy Example then, no more
In moulds of Clay will I my God adore;
But teare those Idols from my Heart, and Write
What his blest Sp'rit, not fond Love, shall endite.
Then, I no more shall court the Verdant Bay,
But the dry leavelesse Trunk on Golgotha:
And rather strive to gaine from thence one Thorne,
Then all the flourishing Wreathes by Laureats worne.

Tho: Carew.

Maria Wentworth, Thomæ *Comitis* Cleveland *filia præmortua prima, virgineam animam exhaluit An. Dom.— Æt. suæ—*

AND here the precious dust is laid;
Whose purely-tempered Clay was made
So fine, that it the guest betray'd.

Else the soul grew so fast within,
It broke the outward shell of sin,
And so was hatch'd a Cherubin.

In height, it soar'd to God above;
In depth, it did to knowledge move,
And spread in breadth to general love.

Before, a pious duty shin'd
To Parents, courtesie behind,
On either side an equall mind.

Good to the Poor, to kindred dear,
To servants kind, to friendship clear,
To nothing but her self severe.

So though a Virgin, yet a Bride
To every Grace, she justifi'd
A chaste Polygamie, and dy'd.

Learn from hence (Reader) what small trust
We ow this world, where vertue must
Frail as our flesh crumble to dust.

Tho. Carew.

On Shakespear. 1630.

WHat needs my *Shakespear* for his honour'd Bones,
The labour of an age in piled Stones,
Or that his hallow'd reliques should be hid
Under a Star-ypointing *Pyramid*?
Dear son of memory, great heir of Fame,
What need'st thou such weak witnes of thy name?
Thou in our wonder and astonishment
Hast built thy self a live-long Monument.
For whilst toth'shame of slow-endeavouring art,
Thy easie numbers flow, and that each heart
Hath from the leaves of thy unvalu'd Book,
Those Delphick lines with deep impression took,
Then thou our fancy of it self bereaving,
Dost make us Marble with too much conceaving;
And so Sepulcher'd in such pomp dost lie,
That Kings for such a Tomb would wish to die.

John Milton.

An Elegy on Ben. Jonson.

WHo first reform'd our *Stage* with justest *Lawes*,
And was the first best *Judge* in his *owne Cause*?
Who (when his *Actors* trembled for *Applause*)

Could (with a *noble Confidence*) preferre
His *owne*, by right, to a whole *Theater*;
From *Principles* which *he* knew could not *erre*.

Who to *his* FABLE did *his Persons* fitt,
With all the *Properties* of *Art* and *Witt*,
And above all (that could bee *Acted*) *writt*.

Who publique *Follies* did to *covert* drive,
Which *hee* againe could cunningly *retrive*,
Leaving them no *ground* to rest on, and *thrive*.

Heere IONSON lies, *whom* had I nam'd before
In that one *word* alone, I had paid more
Then can be now, when *plentie* makes me *poore*.

John Cleveland.

To the Queen, entertain'd at night by the Countess of Anglesey.

FAire as unshaded Light; or as the Day
In its first birth, when all the Year was *May*;
Sweet, as the Altars smoak, or as the new
Unfolded Bud, sweld by the early dew;
Smooth, as the face of waters first appear'd,
Ere Tides began to strive, or Winds were heard:
Kind as the willing Saints, and calmer farre,
Than in their sleeps forgiven Hermits are:
You that are more, then our discreter feare
Dares praise, with such full Art, what make you here?
Here, where the Summer is so little seen,
That leaves (her cheapest wealth) scarce reach at green,
You come, as if the silver Planet were
Misled a while from her much injur'd Sphere,
And t'ease the travailes of her beames to night,
In this small Lanthorn would contract her light.

Sir William Davenant.

For the Lady Olivia Porter; *a Present upon a* New-years *Day.*

GOe! hunt the whiter Ermine! and present
His wealthy skin, as this dayes Tribute sent
To my *Endimion*'s Love; Though she be farre
More gently smooth, more soft than Ermines are!

Goe! climbe that Rock! and when thou there hast found
A Star, contracted in a Diamond,
Give it *Endimion*'s Love, whose glorious Eyes,
Darken the starry Jewels of the Skies!
Goe! dive into the Southern Sea! and when
Th'ast found (to trouble the nice sight of Men)
A swelling Pearle; and such whose single worth,
Boasts all the wonders which the Seas bring forth;
Give it *Endimion*'s Love! whose ev'ry Teare,
Would more enrich the skilful Jeweller.
How I command? how slowly they obey?
The churlish *Tartar*, will not hunt to day:
Nor will that lazy, sallow-*Indian* strive
To climbe the Rock, nor that dull *Negro* dive.
Thus Poets like to Kings (by trust deceiv'd)
Give oftner what is heard of, than receiv'd.

Sir William Davenant.

The Grasse-hopper.

To my Noble Friend, Mr. Charles Cotton.

ODE.

OH thou that swing'st upon the waving haire
Of some well-filled Oaten Beard,
Drunke ev'ry night with a Delicious teare
Dropt thee from Heav'n, where now th'art reard.

The Joyes of Earth and Ayre are thine intire,
  That with thy feet and wings dost hop and flye;
And when thy Poppy workes thou dost retire
  To thy Carv'd Acron-bed to lye.

Up with the Day, the Sun thou welcomst then,
  Sportst in the guilt-plats of his Beames,
And all these merry dayes mak'st merry men,
  Thy selfe, and Melancholy streames.

But ah the Sickle! Golden Eares are Cropt;
  Ceres and *Bacchus* bid goodnight;
Sharpe frosty fingers all your Flowr's have topt,
  And what sithes spar'd, Winds shave off quite.

Poore verdant foole! and now green Ice! thy Joys
  Large and as lasting as thy Peirch of Grasse,
Bid us lay in 'gainst Winter Raine, and poize
  Their flouds, with an o'reflowing glasse.

Thou best of *Men* and *Friends!* we will create
  A Genuine Summer in each others breast;
And spite of this cold Time and frosen Fate
  Thaw us a warme seate to our rest.

Our sacred harthes shall burne eternally
  As Vestall Flames; the North-wind, he
Shall strike his frost stretch'd Winges, dissolve and flye
  This *Ætna* in Epitome.

Dropping *December* shall come weeping in,
  Bewayle th' usurping of his Raigne;
But when in show'rs of old Greeke we beginne,
  Shall crie, he hath his Crowne againe!

Night as cleare *Hesper* shall our Tapers whip
  From the light Casements where we play,
And the darke Hagge from her black mantle strip,
  And sticke there everlasting Day.

Thus richer then untempted Kings are we,
  That asking nothing, nothing need:
Though Lord of all what Seas imbrace, yet he
  That wants himselfe, is poore indeed.

Richard Lovelace.

ODE.

Of Wit.

TEll me, O tell, what kind of thing is *Wit*,
    Thou who *Master* art of it.
For the *First matter* loves *Variety* less;
Less *Women* love't, either in *Love* or *Dress*.
    A thousand different shapes it bears,
    Comely in thousand shapes appears.
Yonder we saw it plain; and here 'tis now,
Like *Spirits* in *a Place*, we know not *How*.

London that vents of *false Ware* so much store,
    In no *Ware* deceives us more.
For men led by the *Colour*, and the *Shape*,
Like *Zeuxes Birds* fly to the painted *Grape*;
    Some things do through our Judgment pass
    As through a *Multiplying Glass*.
And sometimes, if the *Object* be too far,
We take a *Falling Meteor* for a *Star*.

Hence 'tis a *Wit* that greatest *word* of *Fame*
    Grows such a common Name.
And *Wits* by our *Creation* they become,
Just so, as *Tit'lar Bishops* made at *Rome.*
    'Tis not a *Tale*, 'tis not a *Jest*
    Admir'd with *Laughter* at a feast,
Nor florid *Talk* which can that *Title* gain;
The *Proofs* of *Wit* for ever must remain.

'Tis not to force some lifeless *Verses* meet
    With their five gowty feet.
All ev'ry where, like *Mans*, must be the *Soul*,
And *Reason* the *Inferior Powers* controul.
    Such were the *Numbers* which could call
    The *Stones* into the *Theban* wall.
Such *Miracles* are ceast; and now we see
No *Towns* or *Houses* rais'd by *Poetrie.*

Yet 'tis not to adorn, and gild each part;
    That shows more *Cost*, then *Art.*
Jewels at *Nose* and *Lips* but ill appear;
Rather then *all things Wit*, let *none* be there.
    Several *Lights* will not be seen,
    If there be nothing else between.
Men doubt, because they stand so thick i'th' skie,
If those be *Stars* which paint the *Galaxie.*

'Tis not when two like words make up one noise;
    Jests for *Dutch Men*, and *English Boys.*
In which who finds out *Wit*, the same may see
In *An'grams* and *Acrostiques Poetrie.*
    Much less can that have any place
    At which a *Virgin* hides her face,
Such *Dross* the *Fire* must purge away; 'tis just
The *Author Blush*, there where the *Reader* must.

'Tis not such *Lines* as almost crack the *Stage*
When *Bajazet* begins to rage.
Nor a tall *Meta'phor* in the *Bombast way*,
Nor the dry chips of short lung'd *Seneca.*
Nor upon all things to obtrude,
And force some odd *Similitude.*
What is it then, which like the *Power Divine*
We only can by *Negatives* define?

In a true piece of *Wit* all things must be,
Yet all things there *agree.*
As in the *Ark*, joyn'd without force or strife,
All *Creatures* dwelt; all *Creatures* that had *Life.*
Or as the *Primitive Forms* of all
(If we compare great things with small)
Which without *Discord* or *Confusion* lie,
In that strange *Mirror* of the *Deitie.*

But *Love* that moulds *One Man* up out of *Two*,
Makes me forget and injure you.
I took *you* for *my self* sure when I thought
That you in any thing were to be *Taught.*
Correct my error with thy Pen;
And if any ask me then,
What thing right *Wit*, and height of *Genius* is,
I'll onely shew your *Lines*, and say, *'Tis This.*

Abraham Cowley.

Against Hope.

HOpe, whose weak *Being* ruin'd is,
Alike if it *succeed*, and if it *miss*;
Whom *Good* or *Ill* does equally confound,
And both the *Horns* of *Fates Dilemma* wound.
Vain *shadow!* which dost vanish quite,
Both at full *Noon*, and perfect *Night!*
The Stars have not a *possibility*
Of blessing Thee;
If things then from their *End* we happy call,
'Tis *Hope* is the most *Hopeless* thing of all.

Hope, thou bold *Taster* of Delight,
Who whilst thou shouldst but *tast*, *devour'st* it quite!
Thou bringst us an *Estate*, yet leav'st us *Poor*,
By clogging it with *Legacies* before!
The *Joys* which we *entire* should wed,
Come *deflowr'd Virgins* to our bed;
Good fortunes without gain imported be,
Such mighty *Custom*'s paid to Thee.
For *Joy*, like *Wine*, kept close does better tast;
If it take air before, its spirits wast.

Hope, Fortunes cheating *Lottery*!
Where for one *prize* an hundred *blanks* there be;
Fond *Archer*, *Hope*, who tak'st thy aim so far,
That still or *short*, or *wide* thine arrows are!
Thin, empty *Cloud*, which th'eye deceives
With shapes that our own *Fancy* gives!
A *Cloud*, which gilt and painted now appears,
But must drop presently in *tears*!
When thy false beams o're *Reasons* light prevail,
By *Ignes fatui* for *North-Stars* we sail.

Brother of *Fear*, more gaily clad!
The *merr'ier Fool* o'th' two, yet quite as *Mad*:
Sire of *Repentance*, *Child* of fond *Desire*!
That blow'st the *Chymicks*, and the *Lovers* fire!
Leading them still insensibly'on
By the strange *witchcraft* of *Anon!*
By *Thee* the one does changing *Nature* through
Her endless *Labyrinths* pursue,
And th' other chases *Woman*, whilst She goes
More ways and turns than *hunted Nature* knows.

Abraham Cowley.

Answer for Hope.

DEar hope! earth's dowry, & heavn's debt!
The entity of those that are not yet.
Subtlest, but surest beeing! Thou by whom
Our nothing has a definition!
Substantiall shade! whose sweet allay
Blends both the noones of night & day.
Fates cannot find out a capacity
Of hurting thee.
From Thee their lean dilemma, with blunt horn,
Shrinkes, as the sick moon from the wholsome morn.
Rich hope! love's legacy, under lock
Of faith! still spending, & still growing stock!
Our crown-land lyes above yet each meal brings
A seemly portion for the sonnes of kings.
Nor will the virgin joyes we wed
Come lesse unbroken to our bed,
Because that from the bridall cheek of blisse
Thou steal'st us down a distant kisse.

Hope's chast stealth harmes no more joye's maidenhead
Then spousall rites prejudge the marriage bed.
  Fair hope! our earlyer heav'n! by thee
Young time is taster to eternity.
Thy generous wine with age growes strong, not sowre.
Nor does it kill thy fruit, to smell thy flowre.
      Thy golden, growing, head never hangs down
      Till in the lappe of loves full noone
It falls; and dyes! o no, it melts away
      As does the dawn into the day.
As lumpes of sugar lose themselves; and twine
Their supple essence with the soul of wine.
  Fortune? alas, above the world's low warres
Hope walks; & kickes the curld heads of conspiring starres.
Her keel cutts not the waves where These winds stirr,
Fortune's whole lottery is one blank to her.
      Sweet hope! kind cheat! fair fallacy by thee
      We are not WHERE nor What we be,
But WHAT & WHERE we would be. Thus art thou
Our absent PRESENCE, and our future Now.
Faith's sister! nurse of fair desire!
Fear's antidote! a wise & well-stay'd fire!
Temper twixt chill despair, & torrid joy!
Queen Regent in yonge love's minority!
      Though the vext chymick vainly chases
      His fugitive gold through all her faces;
Though love's more feirce, more fruitlesse, fires assay
    One face more fugitive then all they;
True hope's a glorious hunter & her chase,
The GOD of nature in the feilds of grace.

VIVE JESU.

Richard Crashaw.

On the Death of Mr. Crashaw.

POet and *Saint*! to thee alone are given
The two most sacred *Names* of *Earth* and *Heaven.*
The hard and rarest *Union* which can be
Next that of *Godhead* with *Humanitie.*
Long did the *Muses* banisht *Slaves* abide,
And built vain *Pyramids* to mortal pride;
Like *Moses* Thou (though Spells and Charms withstand)
Hast brought them nobly home back to their *Holy Land.*
    Ah wretched *We*, *Poets* of *Earth*! but *Thou*
Wert *Living* the same *Poet* which thou'rt *Now,*
Whilst *Angels* sing to thee their ayres divine,
And joy in an applause so great as *thine.*
Equal society with them to hold,
Thou need'st not make *new Songs*, but say the *Old.*
And they (kind Spirits!) shall all reioyce to see
How little less then *They*, *Exalted Man* may be.
Still the old *Heathen Gods* in *Numbers* dwell,
The *Heav'enliest* thing on Earth still keeps up *Hell.*
Nor have we yet quite purg'd the *Christian Land*;
Still *Idols* here, like *Calves* at *Bethel* stand.
And though *Pans Death* long since all *Oracles* broke,
Yet still in Rhyme the *Fiend Apollo* spoke:
Nay with the worst of Heathen dotage We
(Vain men!) the *Monster Woman Deifie*;
Find *Stars*, and tye our *Fates* there in a *Face*,
And *Paradise* in them by whom we *lost* it, place.
What different faults corrupt our *Muses* thus?
Wanton as *Girles*, as *old Wives*, *Fabulous*!
    Thy spotless *Muse*, like *Mary*, did contain
The boundless *Godhead*; she did well disdain

That her *eternal Verse* employ'd should be
On a less subject then *Eternitie*;
And for a sacred *Mistress* scorn'd to take,
But her whom *God* himself scorn'd not his *Spouse* to make.
It (in a kind) *her Miracle* did do;
A fruitful *Mother* was, and *Virgin* too.
How well (blest Swan) did Fate contrive thy death;
And made thee render up thy tuneful breath
In thy great *Mistress* Arms? thou most divine
And richest *Off'ering* of *Loretto's Shrine*!
Where like some holy *Sacrifice* t'expire,
A *Fever* burns thee, and *Love* lights the *Fire*.
Angels (they say) brought the fam'ed *Chappel* there,
And bore the sacred Load in Triumph through the air.
'Tis surer much they brought thee there, and *They*,
And *Thou*, their charge, went *singing* all the way.
Pardon, my *Mother Church*, if I consent
That *Angels* led him when from thee he went,
For even in *Error* sure no *Danger* is
When joyn'd with so much *Piety* as *His*.
Ah, mighty *God*, with shame I speak't, and grief,
Ah that our greatest *Faults* were in *Belief*!
And our weak *Reason* were ev'en weaker yet,
Rather then thus our *Wills* too strong for it.
His *Faith* perhaps in some nice Tenents might
Be wrong; his *Life*, I'm sure, was *in the right*.
And I my self a *Catholick* will be,
So far at least, great *Saint*, to *Pray* to thee.
Hail, *Bard Triumphant*! and some care bestow
On *us*, the *Poets Militant* Below!
Oppos'ed by our old En'emy, adverse *Chance*,
Attacqu'ed by *Envy*, and by *Ignorance*,
Enchain'd by *Beauty*, tortur'd by *Desires*,

Expos'd by *Tyrant-Love* to savage *Beasts* and *Fires*.
Thou from low earth in nobler *Flames* didst rise,
And like *Elijah*, mount *Alive* the skies.
Elisha-like (but with a wish much less,
More fit thy *Greatness*, and my *Littleness*)
Lo here I beg (I whom thou once didst prove
So humble to *Esteem*, so Good to *Love*)
Not that thy *Spirit* might on me *Doubled* be,
I ask but *Half* thy mighty *Spirit* for Me.
And when my *Muse* soars with so strong a Wing,
'Twill learn of things *Divine*, and first of *Thee* to sing.

Abraham Cowley.

Destinie.

Hoc quoq; Fatale est sic ipsum expendere Fatum. Manil.

STrange and *unnatural!* lets stay and see
This *Pageant* of a *Prodigie.*
Lo, of themselves th'enlivened *Chesmen* move,
Lo, the unbred, ill-organ'd *Pieces* prove,
As full of *Art*, and *Industrie*,
Of *Courage* and of *Policie*,
As *we our selves* who think ther's nothing *Wise* but *We*.
Here a proud *Pawn* I'admire
That still advancing higher
At top of all became
Another *Thing* and *Name*.
Here I'm amaz'ed at th'actions of a *Knight*,
That does bold wonders in the fight.
Here I the losing party blame
For those false *Moves* that break the *Game*,
That to their *Grave* the *Bag*, the conquered *Pieces* bring,
And above all, th' *ill Conduct* of the *Mated King*.

What e're these *seem*, what e're *Philosophie*
And *Sense* or *Reason* tell (said I)
These Things have *Life*, *Election*, *Libertie*;
'Tis their own *Wisdom* molds their *State*,
Their *Faults* and *Virtues* make their *Fate*.
They do, they do (said I) but strait
Lo from my'enlightned Eyes the Mists and shadows fell
That hinder *Spirits* from being *Visible*.
And, lo, I saw *two Angels* plaid the *Mate*.
With *Man*, alas, no otherwise it proves,
An *unseen Hand* makes all their *Moves*.
And some are *Great*, and some are *Small*,
Some climb to *good*, some from *good Fortune* fall,
Some *Wisemen*, and some *Fools* we call.
Figures, alas, of *Speech*, for *Desti'ny plays us all*.

Me from the *womb* the *Midwife Muse* did take:
She cut my *Navel*, *washt me*, and mine *Head*
With her own *Hands* she *Fashioned*;
She did a *Covenant* with me make,
And *circumcis'ed* my tender *Soul*, and thus she spake,
Thou of my *Church* shalt be,
Hate and *renounce* (said she)
Wealth, *Honor*, *Pleasures*, all the *World* for *Me*
Thou neither great at *Court*, nor in the *War*,
Nor at th' *Exchange* shalt be, nor at the wrangling *Bar*.
Content thy self with the small *Barren Praise*,
That neglected *Verse* does raise.
She spake, and all my years to come
Took their unlucky *Doom*.
Their several ways of *Life* let others *chuse*,
Their several pleasures let them use,
But I was born for *Love*, and for a *Muse*.

With *Fate* what boots it to contend?
Such I *began*, such *am*, and so must *end*.
The *Star* that did my *Being* frame,
Was but a *Lambent Flame*,
And some small *Light* it did dispence,
But neither *Heat* nor *Influence*.
No Matter, *Cowley*, let proud *Fortune* see,
That *thou* canst *her* despise no less then *she* does *Thee*.
Let all her gifts the portion be
Of Folly, Lust, and Flattery,
Fraud, Extortion, Calumnie,
Murder, Infidelitie,
Rebellion and Hypocrisie.
Do Thou nor *grieve* nor *blush* to be,
As all th'inspired *tuneful Men*,
And all thy great *Forefathers* were from *Homer* down to *Ben*.

Abraham Cowley.

Hymn. To Light.

FIrst born of *Chaos*, who so fair didst come
From the old *Negro's* darksome womb!
Which when it saw the lovely Child,
The melancholly Mass put on kind looks and smil'd.

Thou Tide of Glory which no Rest dost know,
But ever Ebb, and ever Flow!
Thou Golden shower of a true *Jove*!
Who does in thee descend, and Heav'n to Earth make Love!

Hail active Natures watchful Life and Health!
Her Joy, her Ornament, and Wealth!
Hail to thy Husband Heat, and Thee!
Thou the worlds beauteous Bride, the lusty Bridegroom He!

Say from what Golden Quivers of the Sky,
Do all thy winged Arrows fly?
Swiftness and Power by Birth are thine:
From thy Great Sire they came, thy Sire the word Divine.

'Tis, I believe, this Archery to show,
That so much cost in Colours thou,
And skill in Painting dost bestow,
Upon thy ancient Arms, the Gawdy Heav'nly Bow.

Swift as light Thoughts their empty Carriere run,
Thy Race is finisht, when begun,
Let a Post-Angel start with Thee,
And Thou the Goal of Earth shalt reach as soon as He:

Thou in the Moons bright Chariot proud and gay,
Dost thy bright wood of Stars survay;
And all the year dost with thee bring
Of thousand flowry Lights thine own Nocturnal Spring.

Thou *Scythian*-like dost round thy Lands above
The Suns gilt Tent for ever move,
And still as thou in pomp dost go
The shining Pageants of the World attend thy show.

Nor amidst all these Triumphs dost thou scorn
The humble Glow-worms to adorn,
And with those living spangles gild,
(O Greatness without Pride!) the Bushes of the Field.

Night, and her ugly Subjects thou dost fright,
And sleep, the lazy Owl of Night;
Asham'd and fearful to appear
They skreen their horrid shapes with the black Hemisphere.

With 'em there hasts, and wildly takes the Alarm,
Of painted Dreams, a busie swarm,
At the first opening of thine eye,
The various Clusters break, the antick Atomes fly

The guilty Serpents, and obscener Beasts
Creep conscious to their secret rests:
Nature to thee does reverence pay,
Ill Omens, and ill Sights removes out of thy way.

At thy appearance, Grief it self is said,
To shake his Wings, and rowse his Head.
And cloudy care has often took
A gentle beamy Smile reflected from thy Look.

At thy appearance, Fear it self grows bold;
Thy Sun-shine melts away his Cold.
Encourag'd at the sight of Thee,
To the cheek Colour comes, and firmness to the knee.

Even Lust the Master of a hardned Face,
Blushes if thou beest in the place,
To darkness' Curtains he retires,
In Sympathizing Night he rowls his smoaky Fires.

When, Goddess, thou liftst up thy wakened Head,
Out of the Mornings purple bed,
Thy Quire of Birds about thee play,
And all the joyful world salutes the rising day.

The Ghosts, and Monster Spirits, that did presume
A Bodies Priv'lege to assume,
Vanish again invisibly,
And Bodies gain agen their visibility.

All the Worlds bravery that delights our Eyes
Is but thy sev'ral Liveries,
Thou the Rich Dy on them bestowest,
Thy nimble Pencil Paints this Landskape as thou go'st.

A Crimson Garment in the Rose thou wear'st;
A Crown of studded Gold thou bear'st,
The Virgin Lillies in their White,
Are clad but with the Lawn of almost Naked Light.

The Violet, springs little Infant, stands,
Girt in thy purple Swadling-bands:
On the fair Tulip thou dost dote;
Thou cloath'st it in a gay and party-colour'd Coat.

With Flame condenst thou dost the Jewels fix,
And solid Colours in it mix:
Flora her self envyes to see
Flowers fairer then her own, and durable as she.

Ah, Goddess! would thou could'st thy hand withhold,
And be less Liberall to Gold;
Didst thou less value to it give,
Of how much care (alas) might'st thou poor Man relieve!

To me the Sun is more delighful farr,
And all fair Dayes much fairer are.
But few, ah wondrous few there be,
Who do not Gold preferr, O Goddess, ev'n to Thee.

Through the soft wayes of Heaven, and Air, and Sea,
Which open all their Pores to Thee;
Like a cleer River thou dost glide,
And with thy Living Stream through the close Channels slide.

But where firm Bodies thy free course oppose,
Gently thy source the Land oreflowes;
Takes there possession, and does make,
Of Colours mingled, Light, a thick and standing Lake.

But the vast Ocean of unbounded Day
In th' Empyræan Heaven does stay.
Thy Rivers, Lakes, and Springs below
From thence took first their Rise, thither at last must Flow.

Abraham Cowley.

On an Houre-glasse.

MY Life is measur'd by this glasse, this glasse
By all those little Sands that thorough passe.
See how they presse, see how they strive, which shall
With greatest speed and greatest quicknesse fall.
See how they raise a little Mount, and then
With their owne weight doe levell it agen.
But when th' have all got thorough, they give o're
Their nimble sliding downe, and move no more.
Just such is man whose houres still forward run,
Being almost finisht ere they are begun;
So perfect nothings, such light blasts are we,
That ere w'are ought at all, we cease to be.
Do what we will, our hasty minutes fly,
And while we sleep, what do we else but die?
How transient are our Joyes, how short their day!
They creepe on towards us, but flie away.
How stinging are our sorrowes! where they gaine
But the least footing, there they will remaine.
How groundlesse are our hopes, how they deceive
Our childish thoughts, and onely sorrow leave!

How reall are our feares! they blast us still,
Still rend us, still with gnawing passions fill;
How senselesse are our wishes, yet how great!
With what toile we pursue them, with what sweat!
Yet most times for our hurts, so small we see,
Like Children crying for some Mercurie.
This gapes for Marriage, yet his fickle head
Knows not what cares waite on a Marriage bed.
This vowes Virginity, yet knowes not what
Lonenesse, griefe, discontent, attends that state.
Desires of wealth anothers wishes hold,
And yet how many have been choak't with Gold?
This onely hunts for honour, yet who shall
Ascend the higher, shall more wretched fall.
This thirsts for knowledge, yet how is it bought
With many a sleeplesse night and racking thought?
This needs will travell, yet how dangers lay
Most secret Ambuscado's in the way?
These triumph in their Beauty, though it shall
Like a pluck't Rose or fading Lillie fall.
Another boasts strong armes, 'las Giants have
By silly Dwarfes been drag'd unto their grave.
These ruffle in rich silke, though ne're so gay,
A well plum'd Peacock is more gay then they.
Poore man, what art! A Tennis ball of Errour,
A Ship of Glasse toss'd in a Sea of terrour,
Issuing in blood and sorrow from the wombe,
Crauling in teares and mourning to the tombe,
How slippery are thy pathes, how sure thy fall,
How art thou Nothing when th' art most of all!

John Hall.

The Exequy.

ACcept thou Shrine of my dead Saint,
Instead of Dirges this complaint;
And for sweet flowres to crown thy hearse,
Receive a strew of weeping verse
From thy griev'd friend, whom thou might'st see
Quite melted into tears for thee.

Dear loss! since thy untimely fate
My task hath been to meditate
On thee, on thee: thou art the book,
The library whereon I look
Though almost blind. For thee (lov'd clay)
I languish out not live the day,
Using no other exercise
But what I practise with mine eyes:
By which wet glasses I find out
How lazily time creeps about
To one that mourns: this, onely this
My exercise and bus'ness is:
So I compute the weary houres
With sighs dissolved into showres.

Nor wonder if my time go thus
Backward and most preposterous;
Thou hast benighted me, thy set
This Eve of blackness did beget,
Who was't my day, (though overcast
Before thou had'st thy Noon-tide past)
And I remember must in tears,
Thou scarce had'st seen so many years

As Day tells houres. By thy cleer Sun
My love and fortune first did run;
But thou wilt never more appear
Folded within my Hemisphear,
Since both thy light and motion
Like a fled Star is fall'n and gon,
And twixt me and my soules dear wish
The earth now interposed is,
Which such a strange eclipse doth make
As ne're was read in Almanake.

I could allow thee for a time
To darken me and my sad Clime,
Were it a month, a year, or ten,
I would thy exile live till then;
And all that space my mirth adjourn,
So thou wouldst promise to return;
And putting off thy ashy shrowd
At length disperse this sorrows cloud.

But woe is me! the longest date
Too narrow is to calculate
These empty hopes: never shall I
Be so much blest as to descry
A glimpse of thee, till that day come
Which shall the earth to cinders doome,
And a fierce Feaver must calcine
The body of this world like thine,
(My Little World!) that fit of fire
Once off, our bodies shall aspire
To our soules bliss: then we shall rise,
And view our selves with cleerer eyes
In that calm Region, where no night
Can hide us from each others sight.

Mean time, thou hast her earth : much good
May my harm do thee. Since it stood
With Heavens will I might not call
Her longer mine, I give thee all
My short-liv'd right and interest
In her, whom living I lov'd best:
With a most free and bounteous grief,
I give thee what I could not keep.
Be kind to her, and prethee look
Thou write into thy Dooms-day book
Each parcell of this Rarity
Which in thy Casket shrin'd doth ly:
See that thou make thy reck'ning streight,
And yield her back again by weight;
For thou must audit on thy trust
Each graine and atome of this dust,
As thou wilt answer *Him* that lent,
Not gave thee my dear Monument.

So close the ground, and 'bout her shade
Black curtains draw, my *Bride* is laid.

Sleep on my *Love* in thy cold bed
Never to be disquieted!
My last good night! Thou wilt not wake
Till I thy fate shall overtake:
Till age, or grief, or sickness, must
Marry my body to that dust
It so much loves; and fill the room
My heart keeps empty in thy Tomb.
Stay for me there; I will not faile
To meet thee in that hollow Vale.
And think not much of my delay;
I am already on the way,

And follow thee with all the speed
Desire can make, or sorrows breed.
Each minute is a short degree,
And ev'ry houre a step towards thee.
At night when I betake to rest,
Next morn I rise neerer my West
Of life, almost by eight houres saile,
Then when sleep breath'd his drowsie gale.

Thus from the Sun my Bottom stears,
And my dayes Compass downward bears:
Nor labour I to stemme the tide
Through which to *Thee* I swiftly glide.

'Tis true, with shame and grief I yield,
Thou like the *Vann* first took'st the field,
And gotten hast the victory
In thus adventuring to dy
Before me, whose more years might crave
A just precedence in the grave.
But heark! My Pulse like a soft Drum
Beats my approach, tells *Thee* I come;
And slow howere my marches be,
I shall at last sit down by *Thee.*

The thought of this bids me go on,
And wait my dissolution
With hope and comfort. *Dear* (forgive
The crime) I am content to live
Divided, with but half a heart,
Till we shall meet and never part.

Henry King.

A Contemplation upon flowers.

BRave flowers, that I could gallant it like you
And be as little vaine,
You come abroad, and make a harmelesse shew,
And to your bedds of Earthe againe ;
You are not proud, you know your birth
For your Embroiderd garments are from Earth :

You doe obey your moneths, and times, but I
Would have it ever springe,
My fate would know noe winter, never dye
Nor thinke of such a thing ;
Oh that I could my bedd of Earth but view
And Smile, and looke as Chearefully as you :

Oh teach me to see Death, and not to feare
But rather to take truce ;
How often have I seene you at a Beere,
And there look fresh and spruce ;
You fragrant flowers then teach me that my breath
Like yours may sweeten, and perfume my Death.

H. Kinge.

On a Drop of Dew.

SEe how the Orient Dew,
Shed from the Bosom of the Morn
Into the blowing Roses,
Yet careless of its Mansion new;
For the clear Region where 'twas born
Round in its self incloses:
And in its little Globes Extent,
Frames as it can its native Element.
How it the purple flow'r does slight,
Scarce touching where it lyes,
But gazing back upon the Skies,
Shines with a mournful Light;
Like its own Tear,
Because so long divided from the Sphear.
Restless it roules and unsecure,
Trembling lest it grow impure:
Till the warm Sun pitty it's Pain,
And to the Skies exhale it back again.
So the Soul, that Drop, that Ray
Of the clear Fountain of Eternal Day,
Could it within the humane flow'r be seen,
Remembring still its former height,
Shuns the sweat leaves and blossoms green;
And, recollecting its own Light,
Does, in its pure and circling thoughts, express
The greater Heaven in an Heaven less.
In how coy a Figure wound,
Every way it turns away:
So the World excluding round,
Yet receiving in the Day.

Dark beneath, but bright above:
Here disdaining, there in Love.
How loose and easie hence to go:
How girt and ready to ascend.
Moving but on a point below,
It all about does upwards bend.
Such did the Manna's sacred Dew destil;
White, and intire, though congeal'd and chill.
Congeal'd on Earth: but does, dissolving, run
Into the Glories of th' Almighty Sun.

Andrew Marvell.

The Garden.

HOw vainly men themselves amaze
To win the Palm, the Oke, or Bayes;
And their uncessant Labours see
Crown'd from some single Herb or Tree,
Whose short and narrow verged Shade
Does prudently their Toyles upbraid;
While all Flow'rs and all Trees do close
To weave the Garlands of repose.

Fair quiet, have I found thee here,
And Innocence thy Sister dear!
Mistaken long, I sought you then
In busie Companies of Men.
Your sacred Plants, if here below,
Only among the Plants will grow.
Society is all but rude,
To this delicious Solitude.

No white nor red was ever seen
So am'rous as this lovely green.
Fond Lovers, cruel as their Flame,
Cut in these Trees their Mistress name.
Little, Alas, they know, or heed,
How far these Beauties Hers exceed!
Fair Trees! where s'eer your barkes I wound,
No Name shall but your own be found.

When we have run our Passions heat,
Love hither makes his best retreat.
The *Gods*, that mortal Beauty chase,
Still in a Tree did end their race.
Apollo hunted *Daphne* so,
Only that She might Laurel grow.
And *Pan* did after *Syrinx* speed,
Not as a Nymph, but for a Reed.

What wond'rous Life in this I lead!
Ripe Apples drop about my head;
The Luscious Clusters of the Vine
Upon my Mouth do crush their Wine;
The Nectaren, and curious Peach,
Into my hands themselves do reach;
Stumbling on Melons, as I pass,
Insnar'd with Flow'rs, I fall on Grass.

Mean while the Mind, from pleasure less,
Withdraws into its happiness:
The Mind, that Ocean where each kind
Does streight its own resemblance find;
Yet it creates, transcending these,
Far other Worlds, and other Seas;
Annihilating all that's made
To a green Thought in a green Shade.

Here at the Fountains sliding foot,
Or at some Fruit-trees mossy root,
Casting the Bodies Vest aside,
My Soul into the boughs does glide:
There like a Bird it sits, and sings,
Then whets, and combs its silver Wings;
And, till prepar'd for longer flight,
Waves in its Plumes the various Light.

Such was that happy Garden-state,
While Man there walk'd without a Mate:
After a Place so pure, and sweet,
What other Help could yet be meet!
But 'twas beyond a Mortal's share
To wander solitary there:
Two Paradises 'twere in one
To live in Paradise alone.

How well the skilful Gardner drew
Of flow'rs and herbes this Dial new;
Where from above the milder Sun
Does through a fragrant Zodiack run;
And, as it works, th' industrious Bee
Computes its time as well as we.
How could such sweet and wholsome Hours
Be reckon'd but with herbs and flow'rs!

Andrew Marvell.

⟨*The Metaphysical Sectarian.*⟩

HE was in *Logick* a great Critick,
Profoundly skill'd in Analytick.
He could distinguish, and divide
A Hair 'twixt *South* and *South-West* side:
On either which he would dispute,
Confute, change hands, and still confute.
He'd undertake to prove by force
Of Argument, a Man's no Horse.
He'd prove a Buzard is no Fowl,
And that a *Lord* may be an Owl;
A Calf an *Alderman*, a Goose a *Justice*,
And Rooks *Committee-men* and *Trustees*.
He'd run in Debt by Disputation,
And pay with Ratiocination.
All this by Syllogism, true
In Mood and Figure, he would do.

For *Rhetorick*, he could not ope
His mouth, but out there flew a Trope:
And when he hapned to break off
I'th middle of his speech, or cough,
H'had hard words, ready to shew why,
And tell what Rules he did it by.
Else when with greatest Art he spoke,
You'd think he talk'd like other folk.
For all a Rhetoricians Rules
Teach nothing but to name his Tools.
His ordinary Rate of Speech
In loftiness of sound was rich,

A *Babylonish* dialect,
Which learned Pedants much affect.
It was a parti-colour'd dress
Of patch'd and pyball'd Languages:
'Twas *English* cut on *Greek* and *Latin*,
Like Fustian heretofore on Sattin.
It had an odd promiscuous Tone,
As if h' had talk'd three parts in one.
Which made some think when he did gabble,
Th' had heard three Labourers of *Babel*;
Or *Cerberus* himself pronounce
A Leash of Languages at once.
This he as volubly would vent,
As if his stock would ne'r be spent.
And truly to support that charge
He had supplies as vast and large.
  For he could coyn or counterfeit
New words with little or no wit:
Words so debas'd and hard, no stone
Was hard enough to touch them on.
And when with hasty noise he spoke 'em,
The Ignorant for currant took 'em,
That had the Orator who once
Did fill his Mouth with Pebble stones
When he harangu'd, but known his Phrase,
He would have us'd no other ways.

In *Mathematicks* he was greater
Then *Tycho Brahe*, or *Erra Pater*:
For he by *Geometrick* scale
Could take the size of *Pots of Ale*;
Resolve by Signes and Tangents straight,
If *Bread* or *Butter* wanted weight;

And wisely tell what hour o'th day
The Clock does strike, by *Algebra.*

Beside he was a shrewd *Philosopher*;
And had read every Text and gloss over:
What e're the crabbed'st Author hath
He understood b'implicit Faith,
What ever *Sceptick* could inquere for;
For every *why* he had a *wherefore*:
Knew more then forty of them do,
As far as words and terms could go.
All which he understood by Rote,
And as occasion serv'd, would quote;
No matter whether right or wrong:
They might be either said or sung.
His Notions fitted things so well,
That which was which he could not tell;
But oftentimes mistook the one
For th'other, as Great Clerks have done.
He could reduce all things to Acts
And knew their Natures by Abstracts,
Where Entity and Quiddity
The Ghosts of defunct Bodies flie;
Where Truth in Person does appear,
Like words congeal'd in Northern Air.
He knew *what's what*, and that's as high
As *Metaphysick* wit can fly.
In *School Divinity* as able
As he that hight *Irrefragable*;
Profound in all the Nominal
And real ways beyond them all,
And with as delicate a Hand
Could twist as tough a Rope of Sand,

And weave fine Cobwebs, fit for skull
That's empty when the Moon is full;
Such as take Lodgings in a Head
That's to be lett unfurnished.
He could raise Scruples dark and nice,
And after solve 'em in a trice:
As if Divinity had catch'd
The Itch, of purpose to be scratch'd;
Or, like a Mountebank, did wound
And stab her self with doubts profound,
Onely to shew with how small pain
The sores of faith are cur'd again;
Although by woful proof we find,
They always leave a Scar behind.
He knew the Seat of Paradise,
Could tell in what degree it lies:
And, as he was dispos'd, could prove it,
Below the Moon, or else above it:
What *Adam* dreamt of when his Bride
Came from her Closet in his side:
Whether the Devil tempted her
By a *High Dutch* Interpreter:
If either of them had a Navel;
Who first made Musick malleable:
Whether the Serpent at the fall
Had cloven Feet, or none at all,
All this without a Gloss or Comment,
He would unriddle in a moment
In proper terms, such as men smatter
When they throw out and miss the matter.

Samuel Butler.

NOTES.

LOVE POEMS.

p. 1. *The good-morrow.*

l. 4. 'The seaven sleepers den'. The seven young men of Ephesus who during the persecution of Diocletian took refuge in a cavern, and having fallen asleep were there entombed (A. D. 250), but were found alive in 479, in the reign of Theodosius. See Baring-Gould's *Lives of the Saints.*

l. 20. 'If our two loves be one', &c. If our two loves are *one*, dissolution is impossible; and the same is true if though *two* they are always alike. What is simple, as God or the soul, cannot be dissolved; nor compounds, e. g. the heavenly bodies, between whose elements there is no contrariety. 'Non enim invenitur corruptio, nisi ubi invenitur contrarietas; generationes enim et corruptiones ex contrariis et in contraria sunt' (Aquinas). 'Too good for mere wit. It contains a deep practical truth, this triplet' (Coleridge).

p. 5. *Sweetest love, I do not goe.*

ll. 6–8. What is probably another arrangement of these lines by the author is found in later editions:

At the last must part 'tis best,
Thus to use myself in jest
By fained deaths to die.

p. 7. *Aire and Angels.*

l. 19. 'Ev'ry thy haire', i. e. 'thy every hair' and 'even thy least hair'. In common use with the superlative;

I say such love is never blind; but rather
Alive to every the minutest spot.

Browning, *Paracelsus.*

ll. 23–4. 'face, and wings Of aire'. Angels who appeared to

men did so by 'assuming' a body of thickened air, like mist (Aquinas, *Summa Theol.* i. 51. 2).

p. 8. *The Anniversarie.*

l. 18. 'inmates', i. e. 'lodgers', not members of the family; sometimes 'foreigners, strangers'.

> So spake the Enemie of Mankind, enclos'd
> In Serpent, Inmate bad.
>
> *Paradise Lost*, ix. 494-5.

l. 22. 'wee no more', &c.: 'wee' is the MS. reading, 'now' that of the editions. 'In heaven we shall indeed be blest, happy; but so will all, equally happy; whereas here on earth we are kings ruling one another, the best of kings ruling the best of subjects.' 'Sir, that all who are happy are equally happy is not true. A peasant and a philosopher may be equally *satisfied*, but not equally *happy*. Happiness consists in the multiplicity of agreeable consciousness. A peasant has not capacity for equal happiness with a philosopher' (Boswell, *Johnson*).

p. 9. *Twicknam garden.* Addressed probably to the Duchess of Bedford, who lived at Twickenham, Donne's patroness and the object of some of his most fervid but enigmatic verses. Compare *A Nocturnall upon St. Lucies Day.*

l. 1. 'Blasted with sighs', &c. 'The very stones of the Chapel,' he wrote once when preaching in Lent to very small congregations, 'break out into foliage and fruit—I am the only dead thing who can bring forth nothing alive' (*Cowley Evangelist*, May 1918. Father Congreve). 'Surrounded', i. e. overflow'd.

l. 17. 'groane', so MSS.; the editions read 'grow'. The reference is to the superstition that the mandrake groaned or shrieked when torn up with a fatal effect to the hearer.

l. 18. 'Or a stone fountaine', &c.

> Nè gia mai neve sotto al sol disparve
> Come io senti' me tutto venir meno
> E farmi una fontana a piè d'un faggio;
> Gran tempo umido tenni quel viaggio.
> Chi udì mai d'uom vero nascer fonte?
>
> Petrarch, *Canz.* xxiii. 115 f.

Some unknown grove
I'll find, where by the miracle of Love
I'll turne a fountain and divide the yeere
By numb'ring every moment with a teere.
Habington, *Castara*, 'To Reason.'

Slow, slow, fresh fount, keep time with my salt teares.
Jonson, *Cynthia's Revells*, I. ii.

p. 10. *The Dreame.*

l. 7. 'Thou art so truth'. Like God, you are not only true, but truth itself.

Io veggio ben che giammai non si sazia
Nostro intelletto, se il ver non lo illustra,
Di fuor dal qual nessun vero si spazia.
Dante, *Paradiso*, iv. 124–7.

ll. 16–17. 'And knew'st my thoughts, beyond', &c. The comma is necessary, for Donne does not say she knew his thoughts *better* than an angel could, but that she read his thoughts directly, which God only, and not the angels, can do.

ll. 27–8. 'Perchance as torches', &c. 'If it [a torch] have never been lighted, it does not easily take light, but it must be bruised and beaten first; if it have been lighted and put out . . . it does easily conceive fire.' (*Fifty Sermons*, 36, p. 332.)

p. 11. *A Valediction: of weeping.* The first is a general title given to several of the poems. 'Of weeping' states the special theme.

l. 9. 'divers', i. e. 'diverse'.

p. 12. *The Message.*

l. 14. 'crosse', i. e. 'cancel'. Editions read 'break'.

Examine well thy beauty with my truth,
And cross my cares, ere greater sums arise.
Daniel, *Delia*, 1.

p. 13. *A nocturnall upon S. Lucies day.*

l. 12. 'every dead thing'. He is the quintessence of all negations, 'absence, darkness, death; things which are not', the quintessence even of that 'first nothing' from which all things are created. 'Of this we will say no more; for this

Nothing, being no creature, is more incomprehensible than all the rest' (Donne, *Essays in Divinity*). The poem illustrates Donne's strength and weakness, his power to produce an intense impression by the most abstract means, here an impression of the sense of nothingness which may overtake one who has lost the central motive of his life. But here and there he refines too much and weakens the effect.

p. 14. *A Valediction: forbidding mourning.* This, like 'Sweetest love', p. 5, and 'Of weeping', p. 11, was written on the occasion of a parting from his wife, perhaps in 1612, when Donne's wife was unwilling to let him go, saying 'her divining soul boded her some ill in his absence'. Donne had a vision of her in the daytime, and sending a messenger home learned that her child had been born dead. 'A copy of verses given by Mr. Donne to his wife at the time he then parted from her. And I beg leave to tell that I have heard critics, learned both in languages and poetry, say that none of the Greek or Latin poets did ever equal them' (Walton). 'An admirable poem which none but Donne could have written. Nothing was ever more admirably made out than the figure of the compass' (Coleridge).

l. 11. 'trepidation of the spheares', i. e. the precession of the equinoxes or movement of the axis of the earth, which has altered our position relative to the various constellations.

p. 16. *The Extasie.* 'I should never find fault with metaphysical poems, were they all like this, or but half as excellent' (Coleridge). The *Oxford Book of Verse* gives some stanzas from this poem, but it must be read as a whole. 'As late as ten years ago I used to seek and find out grand lines and fine stanzas; but my delight has been far greater since it has consisted more in tracing the leading thought throughout the whole. The former is to much like coveting your neighbours' goods; in the latter you merge yourself in the author, you *become He*' (Coleridge).

l. 55. 'forces, sense,' &c. The *συνάμεις*, forces or faculties, of the body, are sense, working on which the soul perceives and conceives.

l. 59. 'Soe soule into the soule may flow', &c. As the

heavenly bodies affect the soul of man through the medium of the air (as was believed), so soul touches soul through the medium of the body.

p. 21. *The Relique.*

l. 27. 'Comming and going, wee', &c.

> The curtesye of England is often to kys.
>
> *Enterlude of Johan the Evangelist.*
>
> What favour hast thou had more then a kisse
> At comming or departing from the Towne?
>
> *Arden of Feversham*, i. 378–9.

p. 22. *The Prohibition.*

l. 18. 'So, these extreames shall neithers office doe'. Of these extremes neither shall discharge its office or function. Compare:

> And each (though enimes to ethers raigne).
>
> Shakespeare, *Sonnets*, XXVIII. 5.

l. 22. 'So shall I, live', &c. Alive, I shall be the stage on which your victories are daily set forth; dead, I shall be only your triumph achieved once, never to be repeated. Compare:

> Great Conquerors greater glory gain
> By Foes in Triumph led, than slain:
> The Lawrels that adorn their brows
> Are pull'd from living, not dead boughs.
>
> Butler, *Hudibras*, I. ii. 1065–8.

p. 23. *Absence.* John Hoskins's poems were lost or destroyed by a Puritan friend of his son in 1653 (Wood, *Athenae Oxonienses*). A few are preserved in *Reliquiæ Wottonianæ* and in MSS.

This poem, which was first attributed in print to Donne in 1711, appeared in Davison's *Poetical Rhapsody* as early as 1602, without any ascription, although Davison was at the time on the outlook for poems by Donne: see Bullen's introduction to his reprint of the *Rhapsody*, p. liii. In a MS. in Drummond's handwriting of poems 'belonging to John Don', i.e. of poems by himself and his friends which Donne possessed and Drummond copied, this poem and another,

> Love is a foolish melancholy, &c.,

are signed J. H. The latter poem is in a Chetham Library MS. (Manchester) and a British Museum MS. ascribed with some others to 'Mr. Hoskins'. Of not many wandering seventeenth-century poems is the authorship so well documented.

p. 24. *On his Mistris, the Queen of Bohemia.*

l. 5. 'What are you when the *Sun* shall rise?' This is the reading of the *Reliquiae Wottonianae*, 1651, and I have let it stand. It gives a less pleasing picture than with 'Moon' for 'Sun', but a sharper antithesis. Compare the Arabian poet Nabigha's address to King Nu'man:

> All other kings are stars and thou a sun:
> When the sun rises, lo! the heavens are bare.
>
> R. A. Nicholson, *A Literary History of the Arabs*, 1907.

But the reading 'moon' appears early, in Este's *Madrigals*, Sixth Set, 1624, and in all the MS. copies of the poem in the British Museum, which Professor Moore Smith has kindly examined for me. The reading 'moon' is better adapted to a woman:

> And all the foule which in his flood did dwell
> Gan flock about these twaine, that did excell
> The rest, so far, as *Cynthia* doth shend
> The lesser starres. Spenser, *Prothalamion*, 119–22.

Another variant is 'passions' for 'Voyces', l. 8, which is also an improvement. But the Madrigal books and MSS. have less justifiable variations. I have therefore reprinted the *Rel. Wot.* version as it stands. My texts are not eclectic. The reading 'Sun' is supported by a phrase in Donne's *Epithalamion . . . on the Lady Elizabeth and Count Palatine*, 1613, possibly the date of Wotton's song. Donne speaks of her as a sun, stanza vii:

> Here lies a shee Sunne, and a hee Moone here,
> She gives the best light to his spheare, &c.

The bolder hyperbole is 'metaphysical'.

pp. 25–6. *Loves Victorie.* From Aurelian Townshend's *Poems and Masks*, ed. E. K. Chambers, Oxford, 1912. The ascription of this and the following poem to Townshend is to some extent conjectural. The Malone MS. 13 (Bodleian), p. 51, and Worcester College MS. 58, p. 237, have many variants in the first of these poems. See E. K. Chambers's edition, pp. 102 and 115.

p. 27. *Elegy over a Tomb.* Dated 1617.

p. 28. *An Ode upon a Question*, &c. The spirit and cadence of this Ode seem to me to echo Donne's *The Extasie*, though the philosophic theme is different. Donne's is a justification of the body as an intermediary in the most spiritual love; Herbert's, a plea for immortality based on the transcendent worth of love. An earlier version of the poem, Professor Moore Smith tells me, is in Add. MS. 37157, British Museum, where the poem is dated 1630.

l. 1. 'her Infant-birth', i.e. probably the snowdrops and earliest flowers. They had faded, and—as though Nature wept for them—a season of rain had followed. I owe this interpretation to Professor Moore Smith.

p. 34. *To my inconstant Mistris.* A characteristically 'metaphysical' variation on the old theme of Wyatt's 'My lute, awake!' Compare with the last stanza Wyatt's:

> Vengeance shall fall on thy disdain
> That mak'st but game of earnest pain;
> Trow not alone under the sun
> Unquit to cause thy lovers plain;
> Although my lute and I have done.

The 'metaphysical' notes are the metaphor of excommunication, apostasy, and damnation; the closely knit logical structure; the vehement close.

Printed from Carew's *Poems*, 1651. The text of Carew's poems needs revision, and the canon reconsideration. See C. L. Powell, 'New Material on Thomas Carew', *Modern Language Review*, July, 1916.

p. 35. *Ingratefull beauty threatned.* A familiar conceit. See Ronsard, Shakespeare, &c.; but the close is Donnean. Compare Elegy vii, 'Nature's lay Ideot, I taught thee to love', and Elegy xix:

> Like pictures, or like books gay coverings made
> For lay-men, are all women thus array'd;

Themselves are mystick books, which only wee
(Whom their imputed grace will dignifie)
Must see reveal'd.

p. 36. *Eternity of Love protested.*

l. 16. 'Shall, like a hallowed Lamp, for ever burn.' Compare:

Now, as in Tullia's tombe one lampe burnt clear
Unchang'd for fifteene hundred yeare.
Donne, *Epithalamion* (Earl of Somerset), xi.

'Why some lamps include in those bodies have burned many hundred years, as that discovered in the Sepulchre of *Tullia*, the sister of *Cicero*, and that of *Olibius* many years after, near *Padua*?' (Sir T. Browne, *Vulgar Errors*, iii. 21.)

'They had a precious composition for *lamps*, amongst the *ancients*, reserved especially for *Tombes*, which kept light for many hundreds of yeares.' (Donne, *Fifty Sermons*, 36, p. 324.)

p. 38. *Ask me no more where Jove bestowes.*

l. 11. 'dividing throat', i. e. 'descanting', 'warbling'. 'Division' is 'the execution of a rapid melodic passage'. One seems to hear and see Celia executing elaborate trills as Carew sits entranced.

p. 39. *To Roses in the bosome of Castara.* From Habington's *Castara, The first Part*, 1634.

p. 40. *Of thee (kind boy).* From *Fragmenta Aurea. A Collection of all the Incomparable Peeces, written by Sir John Suckling*, 1646.

p. 41. *Oh! for some honest Lovers ghost.* Compare Donne's *Loves Deitie* (*Poems*, Oxford, 1912, i, 54):

I long to talke with some old lovers ghost, &c.

p. 43. *Out upon it, I have lov'd.* From *The Last Remains of Sr John Suckling*, 1659.

p. 44. *To Cynthia.* From Kynaston's *Leoline and Sydanis. With sundry affectionate addresses to his mistresse, under the name of Cynthia*, 1642 ('Cynthiades', pp. 48–9).

p. 45. *Noe more unto my thoughts appeare.* This and the next poem are from Malone MS. 13, (Bodleian) pp. 65, 83.

p. 49. *The Lark now leaves his watry Nest.* From Davenant's *Works*, 1673.

ll. 11–12. 'Awake, awake, break through', &c. Compare:

> Others neare you shall whispering speake,
> And wagers lay, at which side day will breake,
> And win by observing, then, whose hand it is
> That opens first a curtaine, hers or his.
> Donne, *Epithalamion . . . on the Lady Elizabeth*, &c.

In l. 4, 1673 reads 'to implore'; and in the next poem, l. 22, 'all her Lovers'.

p. 51. *Loves Horoscope.* From *Steps to the Temple. Sacred Poems, with other Delights of the Muses*, 1646, 1648.

l. 25. 'twin'd upon', were united on. Compare:

> true Libertie
> Is lost, which alwayes with right Reason dwells
> Twinn'd, and from her hath no dividual being.
> *Paradise Lost*, xii. 85.

p. 53. *Wishes. To his (supposed) Mistresse.*

l. 70. 'fond and slight'. This is the reading of Harl. MSS. 6917–8 (British Museum). The 'flight' of all the editions is a printer's error, an easy error if one recalls the long 's'. The MS. spelling is 'sleight'.

p. 57. *To Lucasta, Going beyond the Seas.* From Lovelace's *Lucasta*, 1649.

l. 13. 'be 'twixt' for 'betwixt' of *Lucasta* and later editions. This restores the verb.

p. 60. *The Scrutinie.*

l. 12. 'By others'. 'Others may find all joy in thy brown hair, but I must search the black and fair.' The 'In others' of the version in Cotton's *Wits Interpreter* gives a different sense: 'The joy found in thy brown hair may be found elsewhere.' This jars with what follows, spoiling the antithesis.

p. 61. *To Althea.*

l. 7. 'The Birds'. The print of 1649 and one MS. copy read 'The Gods'. The 'Gods' possibly are the birds. Compare Aristophanes, *The Birds*, ll. 685–723, translated by Swinburne, *Studies in Song*.

p. 62. *To Amoret.* From Henry Vaughan's *Poems*, &c., 1646.

ll. 21–2. 'Though fate', &c. An echo of Donne's 'Dull sublunary lovers love', &c. See p. 15.

p. 63. *The Call.* From John Hall's *Poems*, 1646.

p. 64. *An Epicurean Ode*, i.e. an ode suggested by the Epicurean or materialist philosophy.

l. 15. *Terra Lemnia.* A red clay found in Lemnos and reputed an antidote to poison, but also a name for the essential constituent of the philosopher's stone. 'Of what finest clay are you made, of what diamonds your eyes?'

p. 65. *The Repulse.* From Stanley's *Poems*, 1651. With this poem compare Carew's *A Deposition from Love*, pp. 34–5.

p. 67. *La Belle Confidente.*

l. 24. 'marries either's Dust', i.e. 'each marries the other's'. Compare Donne, *The Prohibition*, p. 22, l. 18.

p. 68. *The Divorce.* Compare Donne, *The Expiration*, p. 23.

l. 21. 'woe', i.e. 'woo'.

p. 69. *The Exequies.*

l. 15. 'Vast Griefs'. 'Curae leves loquuntur, ingentes stupent,' Seneca, *Hippolytus*, 604.

p. 70. *Tell me no more how fair she is.* From Henry King's *Poems*, 1657. This may not be King's, but there is no good ground for disfranchising him. Compare Sir William Watson's:

> Bid me no more to other eyes,
> With wandering worship fare, &c. *Odes, &c.*, 1895.

p. 70. *The Spring.* From Cowley's *Works*, 1668. Cp. this with Donne's *To the Countesse of Bedford*, 'Madame, You have refin'd mee' (*Poems*, Oxford, 1912, i, 191–3), a characteristically different treatment of much the same theme; e.g. ll. 47–8 with Donne's:

to this place
You are the season (Madame) you the day,
'Tis but a grave of spices, till your face
Exhale them, and a thick close bud display.

p. 72. *The Change.*

l. 7. *Love*'s foes. Professor Moore Smith conjectures 'Fort' for 'Foes', 1668. It seems to me a certain correction.

p. 73. *To his Coy Mistresse.* From Marvell's *Miscellaneous Poems*, 1681.

l. 34. The 1681 edition reads 'glew', which I have with other editions altered to 'dew'. I am told on philological authority that 'glew' *may* stand for 'glow'. I shall accept that view when convinced by other examples that a seventeenth-century reader would so have understood it. My own view is that if 'glew' be the right reading, it stands for 'glue' as in 'cherry-tree glue', 'plum-tree glue', and that Marvell thought of the dew as an exhalation:

And while thy willing Soul transpires
At every pore with instant Fires.

But 'morning dew' is a frequent combination; and 'dew' suggests at once moisture and glow. Compare:

pleasant the Sun
When first on this delightful Land he spreads
His orient Beams, on herb, tree, fruit, and flour,
Glistring with dew. *Paradise Lost*, iv. 642–5.

l. 40. 'slow-chapt', i. e. slow-devouring. The chaps, Scottish 'chafts', are the jaws.

p. 75. *The Gallery.*

l. 42. 'does' for 'dost' 1681.

l. 48. Marvell may have changed 'are' to 'were' when the Commonwealth had sold Charles I's pictures. See Clarendon, *History of the Rebellion*, xi. 251.

p. 80. *To my Excellent Lucasia.* From *Poems by the most deservedly Admired M^rs. Katherine Philips, The Matchless Orinda*, 1667.

DIVINE POEMS.

p. 85. All the poems by Donne given here (except *Good-friday*, 1613. *Riding Westward*) were written after the death of his wife in 1617, and are eloquent of sorrow and remorse. Conceits and ruggedness notwithstanding, they may be read with the great penitentiary psalms.

p. 85. *Holy Sonnets.—Thou hast made me*, &c.

l. 3. 'I runne to death', &c. I am weary of my groaning; every night wash I my bed: and water my couch with my tears, &c. (Psalms vi. 6.)

ll. 7–8. 'my feeble flesh doth waste By sinne in it', &c. There is no health in my flesh, because of thy displeasure: neither is there any rest in my bones, by reason of my sin, &c. (Psalms xxxviii. 3, &c.)

p. 86. *This is my playes last scene.* Donne had been in his youth 'a great Visiter of Ladies, a great Frequenter of Plays, a great Writer of conceited Verses' (Richard Baker, *Chronicle of the Kings of England*). In the sermons Donne speaks of 'the obscenities and scurrilities of a Comedy, or the drums and ejulations of a Tragedie'.

l. 13. Impute me righteous'. 'God promiseth to forgive us our sins and to impute us for full righteous' (Tyndale). This construction is obsolete. The regular use is as in: 'David describeth the blessed fulness of that man unto whom God imputeth righteousness without deeds' (Romans iv. 6 (Great Bible)).

p. 89. *Goodfriday*, 1613. *Riding Westward.*

l. 1. The different spheres of heaven in the old astronomy were each moved and directed by an Intelligence or Angel. Each of the spheres after the first, the Primum Mobile, has its own movement, but is also affected by the others; hence the (as it seemed) erratic movements of the planets. So our souls, which should follow God's law, admit pleasure and business as their chief motives.

l. 10. 'my Soules forme', i. e. essence, true nature.

20. 'and the Sunne winke':

Era il giorno ch'al sol si scoloraro,
Per la pietà del suo fattore, i rai. Petrarch, *Canz.* 3.

l. 22. 'turne' *MSS.*: 'tune' *Edd.*, which is perhaps right; but the chief idea here is of God's power.

l. 24. 'Zenith to us,' &c., i. e., apparently, 'height so infinite that for Him the difference between us and our antipodes is non-existent. He is zenith to both.'

p. 91. *Hymne to God.* This was written, as Sir Julius Caesar's copy (Add. MS. 34324, Brit. Mus.) states, during Donne's sickness in 1623, when he composed his *Devotions upon Emergent Occasions, and severall steps in my Sickness*, 1624. Walton wrongly assigns its composition to Donne's last illness in 1630.

l. 16. 'Is the Pacifique Sea', &c. 'Be my home in the Pacific, or in the East Indies, or in Jerusalem,—to each I must sail through a strait, viz. Anyan (i. e. Behring) Strait if I go west by the North-West passage, or Magellan (for the route round Cape Horn was unknown), or Gibraltar.'

l. 22. '*Christs* Crosse, and *Adams* tree'. An old belief.

p. 94. *A Dialogue*, &c. *Reliquiæ Wottonianæ*, 1651, signed 'Ignoto'.

p. 95. *On the morning of Christs Nativity.* From Milton's *Poems*, 1645.

l. 74. 'Lucifer', i. e. Venus, the Morning Star, and in the Evening, Hesperus:

Sweet Hesper-Phosphor, double name
For what is one. Tennyson, *In Memoriam.*

l. 91. 'Perhaps their loves', &c. Milton thinks of them as the shepherds of Pastoral Poetry.

l. 92. 'silly', i. e. innocent.

l. 102. 'Beneath the hollow round . . . the Airy region.' The air extended, in the old philosophy, from the earth to the moon, where the region of fire began; 'thrilling', i. e. piercing.

l. 116. 'unexpressive', i. e. not to be expressed or described.

l. 119. 'But when of old', &c. 'When the morning stars sang together, and all the sons of God shouted for joy.' Job xxxviii. 7.

l. 131. 'ninefold harmony', i. e. 'harmony of the nine spheres' (Plato, *Republic*, 10).

l. 139. 'Hell it self', &c. Milton at this period thinks of Hell as in the centre of the earth. So Dante. In *Paradise Lost* it is further removed.

l. 143. 'Th'enameld *Arras*', i.e. variegated tissue. In 1673 altered to

> Orb'd in a Rain-bow; and like glories wearing
> Mercy will sit between.

l. 155. 'ychain'd'. A Spenserian archaism.

l. 172. 'Swindges the scaly Horrour'. So Spenser of the dragon on which Duessa rode; 'Scourging th' emptie ayre with his long traine' (*Faerie Queene*, I. viii. 17). These grotesque figures have disappeared in *Paradise Lost*.

l. 191. '*Lars* and *Lemures*'. Household Gods.

l. 194. 'service quaint', i. e. elaborate ritual.

ll. 197–228. Compare *Paradise Lost*, I. 392–521.

l. 215. 'unshowr'd Grasse'. No rain falls in Egypt.

l. 227. 'Our Babe', &c. As Hercules in his cradle strangled the serpents.

ll. 235–6. 'And the yellow-skirted *Fayes*', &c. Milton had read *A Midsummer-Night's Dream*:

> Then my queen, in silence sad,
> Trip we after night's shade, &c. (IV. i. 101).

p. 103. *Redemption.* From *The Temple. Sacred Poems and Private Ejaculations*, 1633.

l. 12. 'ragged', i. e. rugged, rough.

p. 105. *Affliction.*

l. 53. 'crosse-bias me', i. e. give me an inclination other than my own.

p. 107. *Jordan.* A protest, it is said, against love poems, but also, I think, against the pastoral allegorical poetry of the Cambridge Spenserians.

p. 108. *The Church-floore*, as a type of the Christian life.

p. 108. *The Windows.*

l. 6. 'anneal', i.e. fix the colours by heating the glass. With the whole poem compare the missionary poet, A. S. Cripps's *All Saints' Day* in *Lyra Evangelistica*, Blackwell, Oxford, 1911:

Ah me!
It was God's choice ere mine that I should be
The one dim casement by whose panes they see,
These maiden knights of mine,—their elders' chivalry!
. . . .

Behold!
At my poor breath-dimm'd panes what pomps unfold!
See the Host rise a Harvest Moon of gold!
Lo the Vine's Branches bend with clusters yet untold!

Ah me!
Flawed priest, that God should choose to make of thee
A nursery window, whence his babes may see
Rapture of Saints that are, wonder of Saints to be!

p. 109. *Vertue.*
l. 11. 'closes', i. e. the cadences or conclusions of musical phrases.

p. 111. *Jesu.* 'J' and 'I' must be read as the same letter. '*I* in the other power is meerely an other Letter, and would aske to enjoy an other *Character*. For, where it leads the sounding *Vowell*, and beginneth the Syllabe, it is ever a *Consonant*: as in *James*, *John*, . . . having the force of . . . the *Italians Gi*' (Ben Jonson, *English Grammar*).

p. 111. *The Collar*, i. e. the inhibitions of conscience and God's Spirit. Herbert compares the waiter on God's will to the suitor at Court.

p. 112. *Aaron.* See Exodus xxviii. 2 f. 'And thou shalt make holy garments for Aaron thy brother', &c.

l. 2. 'Light and perfections'. 'And thou shalt put in the breastplate of judgement the Urim and the Thummim', &c. (Exodus xxviii. 30). *Marginal note*, 'That is the Lights and the Perfections'.

l. 3. 'Harmonious bells'. 'A golden bell and a pomegranate upon the skirts of the robe round about' (Exodus xxviii. 33–5). Hence Browning's 'Bells and Pomegranates'. Each verse of

Herbert's poem suggests metrically the swelling and dying sound of a bell; and, like a bell, the rhymes reiterate the same sound.

p. 115. *Why dost thou shade thy lovely face?* From *Emblemes* by Francis Quarles, 1635, Book III. viii. This poem is parodied by Rochester. See *Oxford Book of Verse*, No. 416. l. 37. 'to tine', i. e. 'to kindle'. OE. *tyndan*. The commoner dialectal form is 'tind'.

p. 117. *Ev'n like two little bank-dividing brookes*. *Emblemes*, V. iii.

p. 119. *When I survay the bright Cœlestiall spheare*. From *Castara*, *The Third Part*, 1640. 'Nox nocti indicat scientiam' —Psalms xviii. 3 (Vulgate), xix. 2 (Authorized Version).

p. 121. *Lord when the wise men*, &c. From Malone MS. 13 (Bodleian), pp. 84–5.

p. 122. *To the Countesse of Denbigh*. From *Carmen Deo Nostro, Te Decet Hymnus, Sacred Poems, Collected, Corrected, Augmented*, Paris, 1652. I have followed this text, in this and the following poems by Crashaw, with some corrections from edd. 1646, 1648. The French printer adopts for the article 'a' the form for the French preposition 'à'.

The Countesse of Denbigh is, I suppose, the sister of the Duke of Buckingham and wife of William Feilding, first Earl. The second Earl took the side of the Parliament, though half-heartedly.

p. 124. *Hymn of the Nativity*. There are several variants in 1646, 1648, of which the most interesting is a stanza after l. 90:

Shee sings thy Teares asleepe, and dips
Her Kisses in thy weeping Eye,
She spreads the red leaves of thy Lips
That in their Buds yet blushing lye,
She 'gainst those Mother-Diamonds tryes
The points of her young Eagles Eyes.

p. 128. *Hymn in Adoration of the Blessed Sacrament*. In 1648, where this poem first appears, the title is *A Hymne to Our Saviour by the Faithfull Receiver of the Sacrament*.

I have corrected a few errors of the Paris printer of 1652

from earlier editions, e.g. l. 33, 'Help, lord, my Faith, thy Hope increase', where 1652 drops 'my Faith'

p. 130. *The Weeper.* This is the title in 1646, 1648. The poem is headed by a couplet:

Loe where a Wounded Heart with Bleeding Eyes conspire,
Is she a Flaming Fountain, or a Weeping fire?

l. 2. 'sylver-footed'. The editions of 1646, 1648, and Addit. MS. 33219 read 'silver-forded', i.e. with silver fords, but 'silver-footed' personifies the rills.

l. 23. 'Waters above th'Heavns', &c. What the 'waters above the firmament' (Genesis i. 7) were was a difficult problem for Catholic philosophy. See Donne's *Poems* (Oxford), ii. 210.

l. 71. 'draw' 1648 and Sancroft MS., 'deaw' 1651.

p. 137. *Hymn to Saint Teresa.* First title was 'In memory of the Vertuous and Learned Lady Madre de Teresa that sought an Early Martyrdome'. For the martyrdom see George Eliot, *Middlemarch*, Prelude.

p. 142. *Regeneration.* From Henry Vaughan's *Silex Scintillans: Or Sacred Poems and Private Ejaculations*, 1650, 1655. A symbolic parable on the theme: 'The wind bloweth where it listeth, and thou hearest the voice thereof, but knowest not whence it cometh, and whither it goeth; so is every one that is born of the Spirit' (John iii. 8). The descriptions of nature have the freshness, the suggestion of drawing straight from life, which is all Vaughan's own in his century. There is no suspicion of conventional pastoralism or decoration. The closest parallel, in the poetry of the century, is found in some of the nature pieces of the Dutch poet Vondel.

p. 148. *Man.* This and the previous poem contain the essence of the thought which Wordsworth returned to with such imaginative passion after the storm and stress of revolutionary hopes and disappointments. The life of nature, of natural things, trees and flowers and rivers and mountains and birds and beasts, is in some way right, in harmony with the Divine will, as Man's life is not. In them natural impulse and natural inhibition have harmonized, and their life is full of content and joy:

> If this belief from Heaven be sent,
>   If such be Nature's holy plan,
> Have I not reason to lament
>   What man has made of man?

Modern feeling has moved away from such confidence, which was a development of the doctrine of the Fall. The life of natural things too, we sadly recognize, is full of effort and failure: 'Here as everywhere the Unfulfilled Intention, which makes life what it is, was as obvious as it could be among the depraved crowds of a city slum. The leaf was deformed, the curve was crippled, the taper was interrupted; the lichen ate the vigour of the stalk and the ivy slowly strangled to death the promising sapling' (Thomas Hardy, *The Woodlanders*.).

p. 152. *The dwelling-place.* The verses of St. John are: 'And they said unto him, Rabbi . . . where abidest thou? He saith unto them, Come, and ye shall see. They came therefore and saw where he abode; and they abode with him that day'.

p. 152. *The Night.* 'The same came unto him by night' (John iii. 2).

l. 29. '*Christs* progress'. A marginal note in the 1650 edition refers to: 'And in the morning, a great while before day, he rose up and went out, and departed into a desert place, and there prayed' (Mark i. 35); and 'And every night he went out, and lodged in the mount that is called the mount of Olives' (Luke xxi. 37).

p. 156. *Quickness.*

l. 5. 'Moon-like toil'. The labour of making the tides rise and fall, to no end. Compare and contrast Keats's last sonnet.

p. 157. *A Pastorall Hymne.* From *The Second Booke of Divine Poems. By J. H.*, 1647.

p. 157. *The proud Egyptian Queen.* From Sherburne's *Salmacis . . . With Severall other Poems and Translations*, 1651 ('Sacra', p. 167) from the Italian of Marino.

p. 158. *The Christians reply to the Phylosopher.*

ll. 5–8. It was believed that a chemist could reconstruct a plant from its ashes. See Browne, *Religio Medici*, Sect. 48.

ll. 17–20. Compare:

> Reason is our Soules left hand, Faith her right,
> By these wee reach divinity.

Donne, *To the Countesse of Bedford* (*Poems*, Oxford, i. 189).

MISCELLANIES.

p. 165. *Elegie. His Picture.* Probably written when Donne with many other young volunteers was going to join the Cadiz or Islands Expedition, 1596–7. See *The Calme* and *The Storme* (*Poems*, Oxford, i. 175–80).

p. 166. *Elegie. On his Mistris.*

l. 23. 'Faire Orithea', i. e. Oreithyia carried off by Boreas. See the magnificent chorus in Swinburne's *Erechtheus*, ll. 555–640.

l. 34. 'Spittles', i. e. Spittals, Hospitals. A street in Aberdeen is called The Spital. A town councillor proposed to change it as being in bad taste! Donne's spelling explains his mistake.

l. 35. 'fuellers', i. e. stokers.

l. 44. 'Gallerie', i. e. entrance-hall or corridor.

p. 168. *Satyre.* Donne's third Satire—a vivid presentation of the choice in religion presented to one like him brought up a Roman Catholic, but becoming intellectually emancipated. Dryden's *Religio Laici* was probably suggested by this poem. Donne was very far at this time from being a convinced Anglican.

l. 17. 'ayd mutinous Dutch', i. e. serve in Holland against the Spaniards. To the Catholic Donne the Dutch are still mutineers.

l. 25. 'limbecks', i. e. alembics, for distilling. Our English bodies are distilled in hot climes.

l. 31. 'Sentinell', &c. Plato, *Phaedo*, 6, &c.

l. 35. 'his whole Realme to be quit', i. e. to be free of his whole realm.

l. 76. 'To adore', &c. Compare *Religio Medici.* I. Sect. 3.

l. 81. 'about must', &c. Compare:

> Or as we see, to aspire some mountain's top
> The way ascends not straight, but imitates
> The subtle foldings of a winter's snake.
> Webster, *The White Devil*, I. ii.

l. 86. 'Hard deeds', &c. Hard deeds are achieved by the body's pains or efforts and hard knowledge attained to by the mind's.

ll. 96–7. Philip of Spain or Pope Gregory, Henry VIII or Martin Luther.

p. 171. *To Sir H. W.*, i. e. Sir Henry Wotton, who went as Ambassador to Venice in 1604. Donne had ruined his own career by his marriage in December 1601.

ll. 21–2. 'To sweare', &c. To sweare love until your rank is such that I must speak of honour not love.

p. 173. *To the Countesse of Bedford.* An example of Donne's metaphysical or transcendental strain of compliment.

l. 1. Honour, Aristotle says, is the greatest of external goods, goods for which we are dependent on others. Virtue belongs to the soul itself. *Nicomachean Ethics* iv. 3. 10.

ll. 10–12. The heat of dung is used for various purposes still, as to crook a walking-stick of hard wood.

l. 19. In whatever obscurity I, who praise you, may live. your glory is communicated to, illumines those who praise you.

l. 27. 'through-shine', i. e. transparent.

l. 29. 'specular stone', i. e. mica, or translucent marble (Pliny, Petronius), of which Donne seems to have read or heard that some temples were once made: 'the heathens served their God in temples *sub dio*, without roofs or coverings, in a free openness; and, where they could, in Temples made of specular stone that was transparent as glass or crystal, so as they which walked without in the streets might see all that was done within'.

l. 34. 'But as our Soules', &c. The human soul includes three souls, that of *growth*, which it shares with plants; of *sense* with animals; *reason*, its human distinction. The first two are first in time, not in 'presidence', i. e. precedence. So discretion, natural wisdom, must yield precedence to religious zeal, though it remains with it, is subsumed not displaced. Compare Davenant, p. 158, ll. 17–20.

ll. 46–7. 'types of God', and so of religion. 'God is a circle whose centre is everywhere and circumference nowhere'.

p. 175. *Farewel ye guilded follies.* Attributed by Walton first to Donne, then to Wotton. One MS. assigns it to King.

ll. 31–2. 'Had I all the wealth of the Indies.'

p. 177. *An Elegie*, &c. Printed from the *Elegies upon the Author* in Donne's *Poems*, 1633. In the 1640 edition of Carew's poems is printed what seems to me an earlier, unrevised version. Some variants are:—l. 5, for 'uncisor'd Churchman' (i. e. carelessly barbered), 'Uncizard Lectr'er'; l. 44, for 'dust, had rak'd' 1640 reads 'dung, had search'd'; l. 50, for 'stubborne', 'troublesome'; and l. 94, for 'Tombe', 'Grave', rejected probably because of the awkward suggestion of 'on thy Grave incise', i. e. 'ingrave'. In 1640 ll. 91–2 are wanting.

l. 87. I read 'thee' for 'the' in all texts. I take the lines to mean: 'I will not draw envy on you by giving a complete catalogue of your virtues'. Compare Jonson's

> To draw no envy (*Shakespeare*) on thy name,
> Am I thus ample to thy Booke, and Fame.

p. 180. *To my worthy friend Mr. George Sandys.* From Sandys, *A Paraphrase upon the Divine Poems*, 1638. It is less correctly printed in Carew's *Poems*, 1640.

p. 181. *Maria Wentworth.* She died in 1632, aged 18, being the daughter of Thomas, Earl of Cleveland, and Anna Crofts, sister of Carew's friend John Crofts.

p. 182. *On Shakespeare.* From Milton's *Poems*, 1645. This epitaph, first printed in the Second Folio of Shakespeare, is quite in the Italian style of wit. Petrarch speaks (*Canz.* cxxxi) of the pure ivory of Laura's face,

> Che fa di marmo chi da presso 'l guarda,

'turns to marble whoever gazes closely at it', i.e. his admiration turns him to a statue. 'We catch,' says Mark Pattison, 'the contagion of the poet's mental attitude. He makes us bow with him before the image of Shakespeare, though there is not a single discriminating epithet to point out in what the greatness which we are made to feel consists.' That is an exact description of the metaphysical fashion in eulogy and in description too. See note on Donne's *Nocturnall upon St. Lucies day*, p. 13.

l. 5. 'son of memory'. The Muses are daughters of Memory.

l. 12. 'Delphick lines', i.e. oracular lines.

p. 183. *An Elegy on Ben. Jonson.* From *Jonsonus Virbius: or The Memory of Ben Johnson. Revived by the Friends of the Muses*, 1638. Signed J. C. It is not quite certain that this poem is by Cleveland. It is not altogether in his style.

p. 184. *For the Lady Olivia Porter.* Endymion Porter was the friend of Herrick also and addressed by him in several poems.

l. 7. 'glorious Eyes' 1673: 'lasting Eyes', *Madagascar with other Poems*, 1648 (2nd ed.).

l. 8. 'Darken . . . Jewels', 1673: 'Outlooke . . . Jewells', 1648.

p. 185. *The Grasse-hopper.* From *Lucasta*, 1649.

l. 8. 'Acron-bed', i.e. Acorn-bed.

ll. 11–12. The capital letter suggests at first sight that 'Melancholy' must be a noun, but it is almost certainly an adjective qualifying 'streams'. See the *Poems of Lovelace*, edited by C. H. Wilkinson.

l. 21. 'Thou best of *Men*', i.e. Charles Cotton. The grasshopper has introduced the address and exhortation. Compare:

dissolve frigus ligna super foco
large reponens atque benignius
deprome quadrimum Sabina,
o Thaliarche, merum diota.

Horace *Od.* i. 9.

ll. 33–6. The order is again obscure. 'Our tapers, clear as Hesperus, shall whip Night from the well-lit Casements where we sport ourselves, and strip her black mantle from the dark Hag and stick in its place everlasting Day.'

l. 37. 'untempted', apparently 'secure, unmolested'.

p. 187. *Of Wit.* Wit is equivalent to imagination, fancy, genius, combined with learning, and showing itself in the discovery of subtle analogies, resemblances. Compare Pope, *Essay on Criticism*, e. g. ll. 290–304; Johnson, *Life of Cowley.*

p. 190. *Against Hope.* These poems illustrate the difference between Cowley's clear, clever wit and Crashaw's warmer fancy. But Cowley's Hope and Crashaw's are not quite the same. Compare Hope in Spenser's *Faerie Queene*, iii. 12. 13, with Speranza in i. 10. 14.

p. 191. *Answer for Hope.* This 1651 text varies as usual from earlier versions, showing revision.

l. 30. 'supple essence' 1652, 'subtile essence' 1646.

p. 193. *On the Death of Mr. Crashaw.*

ll. 37–46. Crashaw died at Loretto, of which he was a Canon.

p. 197. *Hymn. To Light.*

ll. 45–8. Compare Shelley's *Hymn to Apollo*:

> The sunbeams are my shafts, with which I kill
> Deceit, that loves the night and fears the day;
> All men who do or even imagine ill
> Fly me, and from the glory of my ray
> Good minds and open actions take new might,
> Until diminished by the reign of Night.

p. 207. *A Contemplation upon Flowers.* From Harleian MS. 697 (British Museum), where it is signed 'H Kinge'. It is not certain that it is the Bishop's.

p. 208. *On a Drop of Dew.* In the 1681 edition Latin versions of this and the following poem, *The Garden*, are printed immediately after the English. Neither the Latin nor the English can be accurately described as a translation of the other. But a careful reading suggests that the Latin in each case was written first, and served as a guide rather than a text for the beautiful English verses. The relation of the two versions *On a Drop of Dew* and *Ros* is fairly close, though the Latin is at times clearer than the English; e.g. 'Round in its self incloses' (l. 7), means, as the Latin shows, 'incloses itself in its own orb':

> Inque sui nitido conclusa voluminis orbe;

and 'So the World excluding round' (l. 29) is in Latin

> Oppositum mundo claudit ubique latus.

The relation of *The Garden* and *Hortus* is much less close. Portions of the Latin reappear very freely treated, viz. the first three stanzas and the last. Other portions of the Latin are not represented in English, and, on the other hand, stanzas 4–8 read like a happy addition in which the poet has been unfettered by any reference to the Latin. The 1681 editor, indeed, suggests that some of the Latin poem is lost, but this may be an attempt to explain the want of correspondence.

My colleague Professor Oliffe Legh Richmond has read the poems carefully and the opinion I have adopted was suggested by him.

p. 212. *The Metaphysical Sectarian.* The description of Hudibras in Canto I, i.e. on his intellectual side. That of his religion follows:

> For his *Religion* it was fit
> To match his Learning and his Wit:
> 'Twas *Presbyterian* true blew, &c.

l. 12. 'Committee-men'. Committees set up in various counties to fine and imprison malignants.

l. 56. '*Tycho Brahe*,' the Danish mathematician and astronomer. *Erra Pater*, i.e. William Lilly, the English astrologer (1602–81) whom every one consulted.

l. 58. As a justice of peace he could inspect weights and measures.

l. 84. 'Like words congeal'd'. Compare Rabelais, *Pantagruel*, iv. 55

l. 88. 'he that hight *Irrefragable*', Alexander of Hales, d. 1245.

INDEX OF FIRST LINES.